TRUE NORTH

TRUE NORTH

The Yukon and Northwest Territories

William R. Morrison

The

Illustrated

History

of

Canada

Toronto   New York   Oxford
OXFORD UNIVERSITY PRESS
1998

Oxford University Press Canada
70 Wynford Drive Don Mills Ontario M3C 1J9
http://www.oupcan.com

Oxford   New York
Athens   Auckland   Bangkok   Calcutta
Cape Town   Chennai   Dar es Salaam   Delhi
Florence   Hong Kong   Istanbul   Karachi
Kuala Lumpur   Madrid   Melbourne   Mexico City
Mumbai   Nairobi   Paris   Singapore
Tapei   Tokyo   Toronto   Warsaw

and associated companies in
Berlin Ibadan

Oxford is a trade mark of Oxford University Press

Canadian Cataloguing in Publication Data

Morrison, William R. (William Robert), 1942–
    True North: the Yukon and Northwest Territories

(The illustrated history of Canada)
Includes bibliographical references and index
ISBN 0-19541045-9

1. Yukon Territory–History. 2. Northwest Territories–History. I. Title II Series

FC3956.M67 1998   971.9   C98-930127-3
F1090.5.M67 1998

Robert Hood, 'The Hudson's Bay Company Ships *Prince of Wales* and *Eddystone*
bartering with the Eskimos off the Upper Savage Islands, Hudson Strait, Northwest Territories.'
Watercolour, 25.7 X 38.7 cm. W.H. Coverdale Collection of Canadiana, 1819,
National Archives of Canada C-040364.

1 2 3 4 — 01 00 99 98
This book is printed on permanent (acid-free) paper ∞.
Printed in Canada

*To my friends and colleagues at the
University of Northern British Columbia,
who share a northern vision*

TABLE OF CONTENTS

	MAPS	viii
	ABBREVIATIONS	viii
	PREFACE	ix
	ACKNOWLEDGEMENTS	x
Chapter One	IMAGINATION AND REALITY	1
Chapter Two	FIRST PEOPLES	17
Chapter Three	NEWCOMERS	36
Chapter Four	FUR TRADERS AND MISSIONARIES	44
Chapter Five	THE AGE OF EXPLORATION	62
Chapter Six	ELDORADO	78
Chapter Seven	QUIET YEARS, 1900–1940	105
Chapter Eight	INVASION	130
Chapter Nine	THE NEW NORTH	152
Chapter Ten	SEARCH FOR A FUTURE: THE MODERN NORTH, 1970–1995	168
	NOTES	189
	SUGGESTED READINGS	192
	INDEX	196

Maps

Yukon   xi

Northwest Territories   xii

Exploration   63

The Klondike   79

Nunavut   183

Abbreviations

HBC Archives: archives of the Hudson's Bay Company, Winnipeg

NA: US National Archives, Washington, DC

NAC: National Archives of Canada, Ottawa

NWT Archives: archives of the Prince of Wales Northern Heritage Centre, Yellowknife

RCMP photo: courtesy of RCMP headquarters, Ottawa

US Engineers photo: courtesy of the United States Army Corps of Engineers Archives, Fort Belvoir, VA

Yukon Archives: Yukon Territorial Archives, Whitehorse

PREFACE

This book was written in response to a request made by Oxford University Press for a history of the Yukon and Northwest Territories, to be part of a projected multi-volume illustrated history of Canada. Perhaps surprisingly, there is no modern general history of the Canadian North. Morris Zaslow's two volumes,[1] though encyclopaedic in approach and content, cover less than a century, from 1870 to 1967, and although there are many hundreds of books on various aspects of the North, particularly in the area of exploration and discovery, the history of the region has to date been written in piecemeal fashion. The exception is *Canada's Colonies,*[2] by my friend and colleague Ken Coates, which has influenced in many ways the outlook of the present work.

It has not been easy to compress the history of such a region, which is enormous though not heavily populated, into a single short volume, and I will be justly accused of short-changing some of it. This is not a book only on explorers, or missionaries, or Mounted Policemen, or First Nations people—many such books have been written—but on all of the North. What has made it difficult to capture the history of the region is that the Yukon and the two parts of the Northwest Territories, east and west, have for the most part developed along independent, though usually parallel, lines, and thus their history is in fact several histories, each of which could fill a large volume.

The illustrations were chosen for several reasons. Some show famous figures, or famous events, while some depict themes in the text. Others show the face of the land, which is so important to the history of the North, and some I chose simply because I thought they were interesting or beautiful.

For whatever virtues this volume possesses I am indebted to a number of people. Phyllis Wilson, Managing Editor of Oxford University Press Canada, has provided overall guidance to the writers who have taken on this project. Sally Livingston of Victoria was the editor who improved my prose. I should also thank those in various archives who have helped me over the years, particularly the helpful staff of the National Archives in Ottawa, the Yukon Territorial Archives in Whitehorse, and the Prince of Wales Northern

Heritage Centre in Yellowknife. My friend Doug Baker of our university's Environmental Studies Program has helped with his practical northern expertise. My greatest debt, however, is to my wife, Linda, who has put up with my late nights in front of the computer and periodic fits of crankiness for more years than anyone should be asked to.

William R. Morrison,
University of Northern British Columbia,
Prince George,
June 1997

ACKNOWLEDGEMENTS

Excerpt from *Part of the Land, Part of the Water: A History of the Yukon Indians* by Catharine McClellan, © 1987, published by Douglas & McIntyre. Reprinted with the permission of the publisher.

Hugh Keenleyside, excerpt from 'Recent Developments in the Canadian North', speech given at McMaster University, May 1949 from *Sovereignty of Security?: Government Policy in the Canadian North*, Shelagh Grant (Vancouver: University of British Columbia Press, 1988).

Reprinted with permission from The Arctic Institute of North America from *Shield Country: Life and Times of the Oldest Piece of the Planet* by Jamie Bastedo, Komatik Series No. 4, 1994, Calgary, Alberta: The Arctic Institute of North America.

Angela Sidney, excerpt from 'How the World Began: The Story of Crow' from *Life Lived Like a Story: Life Stories of Three Yukon Native Elders*, Judy Cruikshank (Vancouver: University of British Columbia Press, 1990).

From *Ancient People of the Arctic*, Robert McGhee (Vancouver: University of British Columbia Press, 1996).

From *People From Our Side*, Peter Pitseolak (Montreal and Kingston: McGill–Queen's University Press, 1993).

Excerpts from 'The Shooting of Dan McGrew' from *The Collected Poems of Robert Service* (Toronto: McGraw-Hill, 1963). Reprinted by permission of the Estate of Robert Service.

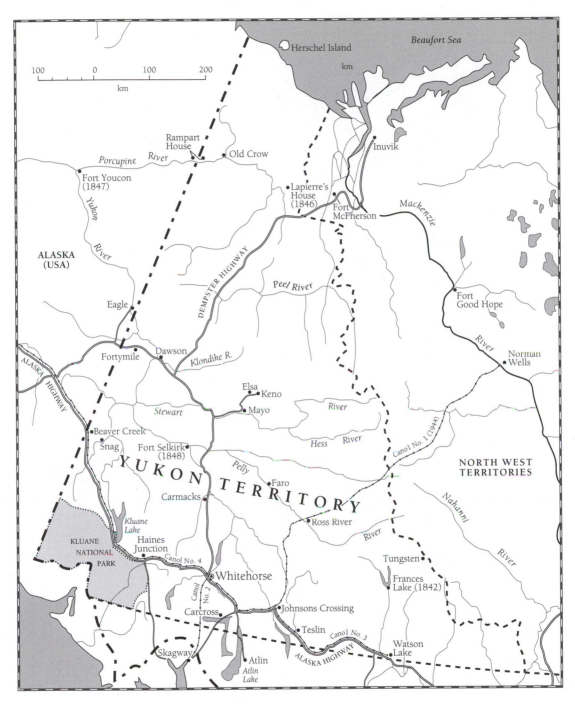

Yukon

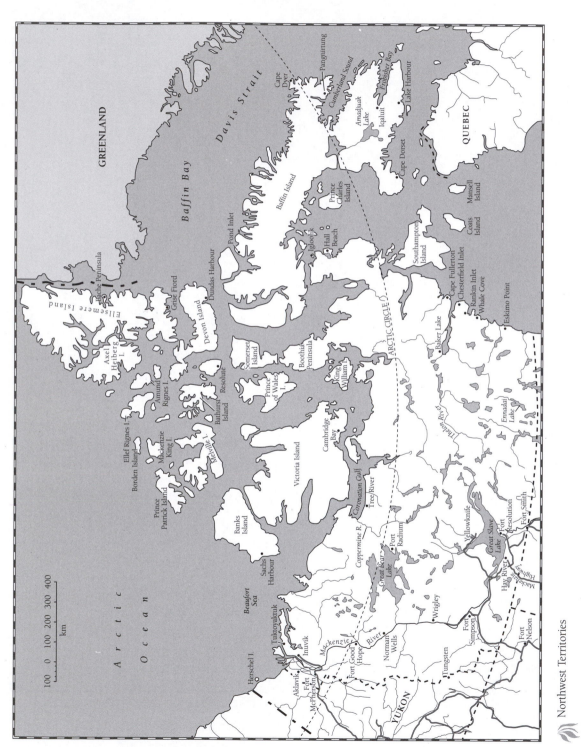

Northwest Territories

CHAPTER ONE

Imagination and Reality

*T*he Canadian North is in some ways not a physical region at all, but a place of dreams, of imagination and fantasy. So few people live in Canada north of the 60th parallel (about 90,000 as of this writing, nearly all of them in settled communities) that the land itself is virtually empty of human life. Few outsiders have visited the region, compared with the numbers who holiday in more benign climates; for most, their experience of the North is confined to the images conveyed by writers, photographers, and film-makers. The picture is an old and generally a bleak one: winter winds keen across the Arctic ice, driving before them thin drifts of needle-sharp ice crystals that pierce through clothing and freeze the skin. A dull red sun hugs the horizon (in fact, in the higher latitudes it hides below the horizon for much of the winter; but this makes the photographer's work more difficult, so we rarely see this part of the picture). In late spring the sun shines twenty-four hours a day and a riot of wildflowers erupts across the landscape. Soon the frost comes, then the snow, and the cycle repeats itself.

When this vision of the North does include a human presence, it is sometimes no more than a suggestion—an igloo, a carving, or an inukshuk (a pile of stones in human form) standing on a lonely point. Or it might be a solitary Inuk crouched motionless on the sea-ice over a seal's breathing hole, waiting to launch his spear in a swift downward thrust; or an ancient grandmother with a tattooed chin, amusing the children with stories and string games on a long winter's night. If the human is a European, it is typically a brave yet doomed explorer—the last of Franklin's men, dying in the snow somewhere near Boothia Peninsula, is the classic example. Farther south the picture might include a fur trader, a gold miner, a missionary, or a stalwart member of the Mounted Police.

Even those who have travelled to the North have read into it what they have needed to see. As I.S. Maclaren, Professor of English at the University of Alberta, has pointed out, the geography of a place—and the North has an abundance of geography—results as much from how we want to see it as from what may actually be there. The nineteenth-century British explorers drew 'aesthetic maps' of the

Mount Logan, located in Kluane National Park in southwestern Yukon, is the highest mountain in Canada at 6,050 metres. Yukon Government photo.

North in their minds, picturing it in one of two ways: either as the 'Sublime', a vast and perilous region inspiring awe and fear; or as the 'Picturesque', a landscape composed in the English manner, fit for colonization and domination by the enterprising British.[1] Both ideas, of course, were imposed on the North by newcomers who needed some comfortable frame of reference to help them cope with a land so vast as to be almost incomprehensible.

The most fundamental view of the character of the Canadian North is the dichotomy expressed by the historian Carl Berger, who observed that to some the North is a frontier, while to others it is a homeland. This was once true of all of Canada, but it is no longer the case outside the North. There, however, the frontier/homeland split is as true today as it was when Martin Frobisher landed on Baffin Island more than four hundred years ago looking for gold. People went north then, and they go now, looking for riches, adventure, opportunities, spiritual regeneration, a blank slate on which to write their own story—whatever it is that they cannot find elsewhere. Hardly a year goes by in which someone does not publish a book telling how their life, their very soul, was irrevocably changed by a canoe trip down the Coppermine or the Thelon; the South Saskatchewan and the Assiniboine, for some rea-

11. A.M.   1.15. P.M.

THE SUN.
DECEMBER 21. 1944.
NORMAN WELLS N.W.T.

This photo, taken at Norman Wells on 21 December 1944, reverses the 'midnight sun' cliché, showing the sun
at noon barely hovering over the horizon. NWT Archives, Jackson Collection, N79-004:0044.

son, do not have the same curative powers. As this chapter is being written, yet another pair of adventurers have returned from a journey on foot to the North Pole, this time unassisted by support planes, and dragging their own sleds; CBC cameras waited at the tip of Ellesmere Island to record the event. For such people, the North continues to be a stage set for their own exploits. For others—and they are not all Native people—the North is a homeland, a place for living, not for adventuring or exploiting. The present book hinges on this dichotomy, for all the people whose lives are contained in it have approached the North in one of these two ways.

How can one come to grips with a region that is so vast—Canada north of the 60th parallel encompasses some 3.9 million square kilometres—and so remote from the centres of modern life? As the twentieth century races to its close, there is hardly a place on earth that is not instantly accessible through modern communications, scarcely a battlefield—Afghanistan, Bosnia, Somalia—that does not appear on our television screens. One may purchase a regular airline ticket to any of these places. But to go to Axel Heiberg Island, or Meighen Island, or Ellef Ringnes Island will require a private charter. The reason is clear enough: these Canadian islands do not sup-

Cape Dorset, NWT, Spring 1968. NWT Archives, Smith Collection, N91-028:0006.

port human life except at military and temporary research stations. Thus they have no wars, no crime, no human tragedy—in short, no civilization—and for that reason they seldom attract the attention of network news reporters. We who live outside the North depend on intermediaries for our knowledge of it: centuries of explorers, artists, photographers, and film-makers. Our lack of first-hand experience of the region makes these images vitally important to our understanding of it.

Yet, whether by necessity or by choice, the images on which we depend generally show only part of the reality. The explorers have emphasized the hardships and the harshness

of the climate; the missionaries, the spiritual darkness of the indigenous inhabitants; the economic promoters, the supposed treasurehouse of mineral riches waiting to be seized. From the early days of European exploration until relatively recently, the images that registered most strongly in the popular imagination evoked terror and hardship—looming glaciers, monstrous bears, perishing cold, ship-crushing sea ice, exotic indigenous people whose lives were, to all but the most perceptive of observers, nasty, brutish, and short.

In many cases these images were reinforced by visual representations. Many of the famous explorers took artists on their expedi-

Deserted whaling building on Herschel Island, the Yukon's first Territorial Park. Yukon Government photo.

tions, and some were competent artists themselves. Certainly many of the later episodes in the region's history, including the Klondike gold rush, were well documented by photographers. Later still the motion-picture camera recorded the building of the Alaska Highway. And, finally, the advent of television brought modern technology to the North, making it possible to broadcast images of the North directly to southerners. In fact, much of the European expansion into the North took place in the era of the photograph, so that in many cases the period of initial contact between Native people and newcomers was documented by the camera to an extent probably unequalled anywhere else in the hemisphere.

Sometimes these photographic images have dispelled old myths. The pictures taken by Robert Peary at the North Pole in 1909 show a flat, almost featureless expanse of snow and ice. Similar pictures could have been taken on the shore of any of the Great Lakes during a severe winter; perhaps it was the banal reality of the actual pole that helped to persuade skeptics that Peary had faked his evidence. Certainly the artists who produced the nineteenth-century engravings of icebergs gave them a menacing look that the camera does not support; photographs of icebergs lack such anthropomorphic qualities. Photographs of

Pond Inlet, NWT, 1968. NWT Archives, Smith Collection, N91-028:0284.

Yukon gold miners at work do not look particularly 'northern'—that is, winter-like—since most of the work was done in the summer, and the image of a Yukon summer is not what outsiders think of as northern. A midwinter picture of a thermometer in Dawson City registering -65 Fahrenheit, on the other hand, certainly reinforces one view of the region.

These images of the Canadian North—four hundred years of word pictures, drawings, paintings, photographs, and films—have to a large extent determined how outsiders would understand the region. Resource developers, potential settlers, writers, even the government officials responsible for its future have in many cases responded not to their own experience of the North, for they have had none, but to the pictures created by writers, painters, and photographers. A modern example of this process is the story of the Inuit of the Keewatin district at the end of the Second World War. Their misery, starvation, and death attracted no particular attention in Ottawa until a young writer named Farley Mowat painted an unforgettable picture of their plight in *People of the Deer* (1952). This book caused much official embarrassment and led not only to quick relief of the immediate problem, but to long-term efforts to ensure that a similar situation would not arise again.

A more recent example is the voyage of the *Manhattan*, an American oil tanker that set out to traverse the Northwest Passage in 1969 in defiance of Canada's claims to sovereignty over Arctic waters. A memorable film about the incident, produced by the National Film Board, caused alarm among Canadian nationalists, many of whom could likely not have located the Northwest Passage on a map.

The visual images that have come from the North can serve as metaphors for northern history. Before the period of contact, images such as bone and ivory carvings, probably used as talismans and reflecting Inuit spiritual beliefs, were produced by northern people for northern people. With the arrival of Europeans, images of the North were produced for outside consumption, to depict the region to the backers of expeditions and the purchasers of their printed records. In this art the indigenous people appeared as curiosities, and the landscape was depicted to look as formidable as possible, an approach that served to emphasize the heroism of the explorers. Images of episodes such as the Klondike gold rush also emphasized human suffering and endurance—the photograph of the line of men straining up the snowy Chilkoot Pass is probably the best-known image of the period. Photographs and films taken of the building of the Alaska Highway during the Second World War depict a heroic band of men taming the wilderness. It is significant that in all these more recent images the indigenous people are marginal at best, and often invisible; the gold rush and the building of the highway were classic 'frontier' episodes that had nothing to do with the North as a homeland, and the Native people were not involved in them.

In our own time, however, the First Nations of the Canadian North are once again producing their own images, interpreting themselves to their own people and to the rest of the world. Nearly forty years ago the Inuit of Cape Dorset, Povungnituk, and a number of other communities began producing prints and carvings that, although aimed at a world market, and influenced by southern artistic tastes, were clearly rooted in their own artistic traditions. Now the Inuit and the Dene of the Yukon and Northwest Territories produce their own television programs, broadcast in their own languages to their people and in English to the rest of the world. As with their images, so with their lives: the indigenous people of northern Canada once answered to no one but themselves; they were 'discovered' by outsiders, subjugated and marginalized; and now they are retaking control.

The post-contact history of the Canadian North has, until very recently, been almost entirely one of frontier exploitation of various kinds, some of it fairly harmless, some less benign. Some of this exploitation was of an easily recognizable variety. One classic example was Clarence Berry, an American who travelled with his wife to the confluence of the Yukon and Klondike rivers at just the right time in 1896, quickly found gold worth more than half a million dollars in the currency of the time, and left the country with his wealth, never to return. Another was Robert Peary, who, in his obsession to be the first human at the North Pole, used the land, the animals, and the people of the North as mere pawns. These are easily identifiable exploiters. But others have used the North in more subtle ways, as a source of images, inspiration, or cautionary tales. In the nineteenth century, for instance, eugenicists and proponents of British imperialism seized on northernness as an explanation of Britain's superiority and a justification for extending its influence. The idea was that the northern climate produced a tough and hardy people, as opposed to the weak, effete products of languid southern climes; thus the law of nature demanded that the former should dominate the latter. The leading Canadian advocate of this idea was George Parkin (1846–1922), a schoolteacher from New Brunswick (and the first biographer of Sir John A. Macdonald) who became leader of the Imperial Federation League, secretary of the Rhodes Scholarship Trust, and eventually a baronet. Parkin believed that the twentieth century would belong to the Anglo-Saxon people formed by the rigours of the northern climate. And since Canada was the pre-eminently northern member of the British Empire, it would necessarily serve as the principal nursery of future imperialists. Similarly, the members of the 'Canada First' movement, though not ardent imperialists, also believed that the Anglo-Saxon race, made especially healthy and vigorous by the bracing Canadian climate, would soon rise to take its rightful place of prominence in the world. The best-known expression of this sentiment appears in Robert Stanley Weir's English version of Canada's national anthem, written in 1908: 'True North, strong and free' encapsulates the pride in Canada's northernness that lay behind the nationalism of the post-Confederation period. Carl Berger described the northern thrust of nineteenth-century nationalism this way:

The adjective 'northern' came to symbolize energy, strength, self-reliance, health, and purity, and its opposite, 'southern', was equated with decay and effeminacy, even libertinism and disease. A lengthy catalogue of desirable national attributes resulting from the climate was compiled. No other weather was so conducive to maintaining health and stimulating robustness. . . . Compared even to the 'warm, moisture-laden atmosphere of the British isles' the sharp and clear air of northern America was calculated to make perception more clear and more penetrating. 'The Canadian is supereminently quick-witted' wrote one observer, because the very air of his country has 'tonic properties'.[2]

The idea that northerners would be the strengthening and distinctive force in the Canadian character has persisted to the present, and the intellectual descendants of George Parkin continue to look to the North for insight and inspiration. After the Second World War, for example, a small group of civil servants and academics, sometimes referred to as 'northern nationalists', pondered the role of the North in post-war Canada. Charles Camsell, former Commissioner of the Northwest Territories, wrote in 1946: 'Just as the map of Canada has for a century been unrolled westward, so now it is northward that "the tide of Empire takes its way." The same racial stock which has carried the flag around the world will also carry it to the farthest north. . . .'[3] The fact that Camsell was part Métis makes this hymn to the Anglo-Saxon race particularly odd.

The most prominent of the northern nationalists was Hugh Keenleyside, appointed deputy minister of Mines and Resources and commissioner of the Northwest Territories in 1946. (That one person could hold both jobs suggests that the responsibilities of the commissioner were still not onerous at that date.) In a speech given in 1949, Keenleyside offered probably the most cogent explanation of what northern enthusiasts saw as the region's place in Canadian life and in the Canadian character. It was a variation of Sir Wilfrid Laurier's statement that the twentieth century would belong to Canada, and a classic expression of the belief that the North was a continuing frontier:

> The frontier is more than a geographical area: it is a way of life, a habit of mind. . . . whereas the frontier in American territory was a phenomenon of the west . . . in Canada the frontier has persisted longest in the North. Here indeed is a true frontier and one that will never be fully conquered.
>
> This is a matter of vital importance to the future of Canada. The virtues peculiar to frontier conditions—social and political democracy, independence and self-reliance, freedom and co-operation, hospitality and social responsibility—are virtues of particular importance in national life.
>
> Perhaps it is here that the greatest contribution will be made by the Canadian North. Much as that area may contribute to the economic life of the country, this contribution may be of less significance than the fact that here will be a permanent source of energy from which Canada will draw strength in the never-ending fight to guard and maintain the personal and human rights of her people. . . . The frontier is a bastion of freedom, and the North is a permanent frontier.[4]

It is not easy to capture cold in a photograph, but this 1915 Dawson City street scene taken at -60 F (-51 C) in ice fog does so successfully. Author's collection.

Keenleyside's North is a philosophical or metaphysical region, and in those terms is fairly easy to define. More difficult is the task of delineating this North on a map. Much ink has been spilled over the decades as students of the North have tried to find an acceptable definition of its geographical limits. The Yukon and the Northwest Territories are political units whose geographical boundaries are highly arbitrary, and it is difficult to argue that Eskimo Point, NWT, is more 'northern' than Churchill, Manitoba, or that Carcross, Yukon, is more northern than Atlin or Fort Nelson,

SS *Pelican* at Lake Harbour, NWT, in 1919. Note the furled sails on the yardarms—steam power came late to the North. NWT Archives, Learmonth Collection., N87-033:0070.

BC. Almost any criterion of northernness that one might choose simply confuses the issue. It is true, for example, that the higher the latitude, the more northerly the location; but this is so only in a purely cartographic sense. In fact, most of the indicators of northerliness in Canada, such as isotherms (lines connecting places of equal temperatures), or the tree line, do not run parallel to the lines of latitude, but diagonally from northwest to southeast. The tree line—the boundary, really a zone rather than a discernible line, between where trees grow on open ground and where they do not—is near Aklavik, almost at the Arctic Ocean, in the Mackenzie River Delta, yet runs southeast to Churchill, Manitoba, before crossing northern Quebec to reach the Atlantic in northern Labrador. Churchill is 1,000 kilometres south of Aklavik by latitude. Polar bears thrive on the high Arctic islands, but they also thrive at Churchill, where they form the basis of a tourist industry. Whitehorse is not materially colder than Prince Albert, Saskatchewan, or even Winnipeg, which lies on the 50th parallel and does not think of itself as northern.

Any attempt to define northernness in terms of latitude or even climate eventually leads to contradictions. In the 1960s the

The Kaskawulsh Glacier, a 25-km hike from the Alaska Highway in Kluane Park. The stripes are caused by rock debris in the ice. Yukon Government photo.

author and businessman Richard Rohmer promoted the development of what he called 'mid-Canada', the region north of the agricultural belt but south of the tree line. His 'mid-Canada concept', like John Diefenbaker's 'northern vision', saw the future of Canada in the development of the mineral and other resource-based wealth of the region. But mid-Canada lay across seven provinces and both territories, and perhaps for this reason the difficulties of translating such a concept into action appeared insurmountable.[5]

Probably the most interesting and useful interpretation of northernness, or 'nordicity', was made by the geographer L.-E. Hamelin in his book *Canadian Nordicity: It's Your North Too*.[6] Hamelin used social as well as physical indicators to construct an index of nordicity—more accurately, an index of 'polar values', or VAPO—that reflects not only climate and landforms but such factors as access to transportation facilities, population, amenities, and public facilities, assigning equal values to latitude, summer heat, annual cold, types of ice, total precipitation, plant cover, accessibility by land, air service, resident population, and economic activities. On this scale the VAPO of the North Pole is 1,000; of

Falls on the Hanbury River, NWT. NAC, PA19565.

Although this is a work of history, not geography or geology, the Yukon and Northwest Territories are so large, and so empty of human life (the population density of the Yukon is 0.06 people per square kilometre, that of the NWT under 0.02; Ontario's, despite its huge unpopulated areas, is 9.7) that no book about the North can ignore the land itself. The area of the two territories is nearly four million square kilometres (1.5 million square miles), and the land that sustains the life of its people dominates that life as well. There is a paradox here, for although northerners live with and by the land, they do not live on it—not permanently, at any rate. The proportion of the population living in communities is thus higher in the territories than in any Canadian province; depending on how one defines a community, the figure can approach 100 per cent.

To put the physical reality of the North into words is remarkably difficult. Lists can be made of its geological features, but the land itself is so overwhelming as to mock any attempt to contain it in language. Barry Lopez, in his excellent and evocative book *Arctic Dreams* (1986), describes the problem:

The physical landscape is baffling in its ability to transcend whatever we would make of it. It is as subtle in its expression as turns of the mind, and larger than our grasp; and yet it is still knowable. The mind, full of curiosity and analysis, disassembles a landscape and then reassembles the pieces—the nod of a flower, the color of the night sky, the murmur of an animal—trying to fathom its geography. At the same time the mind is trying to find its place within the land, to discover a way to dispel its own sense of estrangement.[7]

Churchill, 450; Dawson City, 435; Yellowknife, 390; Keewatin, 812; the town of Verkhoyansk, Siberia, the coldest place in the world outside Antarctica, has a VAPO of 631. By this index it is easy to identify a community such as Baker Lake or Igloolik as northern; but the question of where to draw the line between what is northern and what is not remains a matter of interpretation. In this volume, fortunately, the question does not arise, because it relies on a political definition. The Yukon and Northwest Territories are not the whole North, since they do not include northern Quebec and much of the mid-north, but they are unquestionably northern.

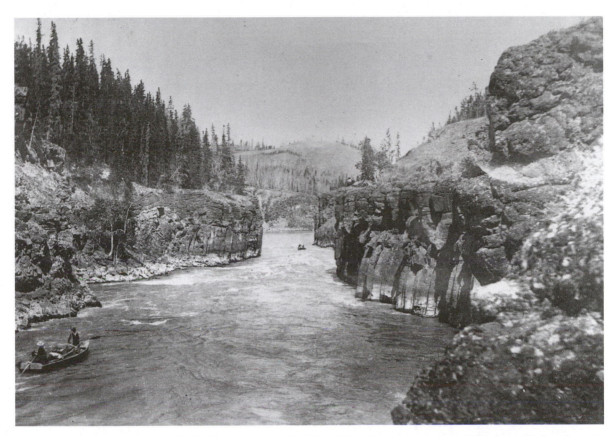

A modern photograph of Miles Canyon on the Yukon River, just upstream from Whitehorse. Before the canyon was partly drowned by a hydroelectric dam, it was a fearsome obstacle to navigation. Over a hundred boats were wrecked and five men drowned in it in the spring of 1898. NAC, C21675.

The North is dominated by the physical feature that dominates all of Canada: the Canadian Shield, 4.6 million square kilometres of Precambrian rock stretching from the Arctic islands north of Hudson Bay to the St Lawrence River east of Kingston and into the Adirondacks of the United States, and from Labrador to the edge of the Mackenzie Valley. The Shield has been a curse as well as a blessing to Canada. The country has no midwest analogous to the American states of Indiana and Illinois, for the Shield stands as a barrier between the rich agricultural lands of southern Ontario and those of Manitoba, and for many years it diverted settlement to the United States instead of the Canadian Prairies. The most difficult part of the Canadian Pacific Railway to construct was not the stretch through the Rockies, though that achievement still gets all the publicity, but the line through the Shield country of northern Ontario, where the surveyors got lost in a maze of rocks and lakes, and the line sank in bottomless muskeg. On the other hand, the Shield blessed the Canadian economy with the fur-bearing animals that were the foundation of the country's

This mastodon head—discovered frozen in the ground at Quartz Creek near Dawson City in 1900—is a reminder of the region's prehistoric past. NAC, PA182827.

early economy, and more recently it has provided a treasure-trove of valuable minerals and forest products. From Kirkland Lake and Sudbury in northern Ontario to Schefferville in Quebec to Yellowknife and Pine Point in the NWT, the Shield has been a mainstay of Canadian prosperity for over a century.

The Canadian Shield is the core of the North American continent. Its rocks are the oldest in the world; a sample of gneiss taken northwest of Yellowknife proved to be 3.962 billion years old. This rock marks an era three-quarters of the way back to the time when the Earth was a cloud of swirling dust and gas; the

only objects on the planet that are older are meteorites. The rock has been deformed and reformed; it has been around the globe several times, floating on great continental plates on a sea of magma; it has been eroded by the elements and scoured by unknown numbers of ice ages. It is unimaginably old; in comparison with it, the Rocky Mountains, only 60 million years old, are mere infants.

It is the Shield as much as the climate that shapes the face of much of the North. Scoured by glacial ice only a few thousand years ago, in the North it is covered by a thin topsoil, underlaid with permafrost, that can support at most

Hudson's Bay Company post, Frobisher Bay, 1939. HBC Archives, N9305.

stunted trees—over large areas, only grass and small bushes. Yet subtle gradations in climate ensure that the region's physical features are by no means uniform. There are also large parts of the North—the Mackenzie River Valley and the Yukon in particular—that lie outside the Shield. But its image is so ingrained in the minds of Canadians that a picture of its topography, wherever taken—in the Barrens of Keewatin (the tundra due north of Manitoba) or the cottage country of Algonquin Park— immediately evokes the idea of 'North'. Jamie Bastedo's excellent *Shield Country* describes its most prominent feature:

In shield country, rock is the ecological bottom line. It determines the lay of the land, the pattern of vegetation, the flow of water. It also dictates patterns of human settlement. . . . Look at a map of the region. A good proportion of the lakes that anyone has bothered to name owe their identity to rocks: Rock Lake, Rocky Lake, Roundrock Lake, Redrock Lake, Rocknest Lake. Many are named after early geologists—rock hounds. They raved about 'the great stretches of clean, bare rock . . . providing ideal conditions for the prospector.' Early non-native visitors to the region were so preoccupied with rocks that the resident Dogribs gave them the name Kwet'i, meaning 'Rock People,' a name that remains very much alive today.

For generations, the rock of the Canadian Shield has played on the imagination of those who call it home, those who stay only a while, even those who have never seen it. It has left its imprint on the nation's best literature, art and drama. It's no wonder.

Almost two-thirds of the country is Canadian Shield.[8]

Perhaps this is why pictures of Dawson City taken in the summer don't look 'northern'—there are no rocks or lakes, and the landscape is only a few thousands rather than hundreds of millions of years old. This is the land, the world's oldest, that supports the Dene and Inuit, some of its youngest peoples.

CHAPTER TWO

First Peoples

For thousands of years the First Nations of northern Canada, like those elsewhere in the Western hemisphere, lived as hunters and gatherers. Archaeologists have, over the years, established the basic history of these people over the ten millennia (or so) before the arrival of Europeans changed everything for them. What has not yet been settled, however, is where they came from, how exactly they got here, and how long ago they arrived. The origins of the Native peoples of northern Canada are enshrined in the central myths of their cultures. Many of these myths tell how humans descended from animals, or came into the world with their assistance. An example is 'The Story of Crow' told by Angela Sidney (1902-91), a Tagish/Tlingit woman of the Deisheetaan (Crow) Clan in the southern Yukon. Like many of these stories, it is quite long, but an extract gives the flavour:

> Then Crow disappears.
> He has those things with him in a box.
> He walks around—comes to a river.
> Lots of animals there—fox, wolf, wolverine, mink, rabbit.

> Everybody's fishing . . .
> That time animals all talk like people talk now—
> The world is dark.
> 'Give me fish,' Crow says.
> No one pays any attention.
> 'Give me fish or I'll bring daylight!'
> They laugh at him.
>
> He's holding a box . . . starts to open it and let one ray out.
> Then they pay attention!
> He opens that box a bit more—they're scared!
> Finally, he opens that daylight box and threw it out.
> Those animals scatter!
> They hide in the bush and turn into animals like now.
> Then the sun, moon, stars, and daylight come out.[1]

Other Aboriginal stories, however, tell of migration. Although some Native people consider modern anthropological explanations to be no less than assaults on their culture, the mainstream theory of how humans came to

Gwitch'in people of the northern Yukon dancing, drawn by the fur trader Alexander Hunter Murray in 1847–48. Author's collection.

the hemisphere—which was first proposed in a Spanish history of the New World published in 1590—is that they travelled from Asia by land over what is now the Bering Strait. This means, of course, that the Canadian North, the last part of the country to be effectively included within the nation state, was the first part of the country to be occupied by humans.

According to this theory, humans walked across from Asia during periods when the sea level was lower than it is now, so that what is now the Bering Strait was dry land. The pathway, known as Beringia, is often referred to as a 'land bridge', but it was actually hundreds of miles wide; in picturing this migration, therefore, one should not envision hardy bands of people crossing a narrow strip of land with the waves crashing on either side, like the Hebrews crossing the Red Sea in the famous film, but a slow and gradual movement in

search of game across what was really a small continent. Thus these people, unlike the others whose descendants live in this hemisphere, would have had no sense of crossing an ocean barrier, of leaving one continent and coming to another: for them, the journey was seamless. It is also possible that they, or some of them, travelled at different times by sea down the west coast of Alaska and Canada, stopping along the way; this would explain the unusual variety of languages along the coast.

What remains a topic of controversy is when this migration took place. It must have been during a period not, as may be thought, when the climate was warm and benign, but rather one when glaciers were active, since it was the formation of glaciers that locked up enough water to make the sea level drop and expose the pathway to North America. This has happened several times since *Homo sapiens* appeared on earth, first about 70,000 BP (before present), and most recently about 14,000 BP. But if glaciers had to be present to form a land bridge, would there not have been an impenetrable ice barrier across northern Canada? The answer is that there was at least one ice-free corridor (probably two) along which people could travel even in the coldest part of the ice age. The existence of such a corridor can be explained by the fact that cold is not the only requirement for the formation of glaciers: the process also requires snow, and parts of the northwest were too dry to permit glaciers to form.

Have humans been in Canada for seventy millennia, or only about fourteen? A good deal of academic blood has been shed over this question, and there is much contradictory evidence. Some experts in linguistics suggest that all the Native languages in the Western hemisphere (there were over 2,000 of them when Columbus arrived) came from a handful of original languages—one scholar suggests only three. Linguists who have worked out formulas showing how long it has been since German and English, or Spanish and Portuguese, diverged from a common root have found that it takes a very long time for languages to change. By such calculations, humans may have been on this continent for thirty or even fifty thousand years.

The trouble with deciding on a date lies in the ambiguity of the archaeological evidence. There is a site in Brazil that suggests a date of 32,000 BP, and one in New Mexico that, according to radio-carbon dating of what may well be the remains of a campfire, is 4,000 years older. But neither site has indisputable evidence of human activity. A good deal of searching has been carried out in the Yukon

A.H. Murray's portrait of a Gwitch'in hunter, with tattooed face. The ornaments, beads, and knife are European. Author's collection.

and Alaska, the area where, if the Beringia theory is true, the first traces of human activity should be found—traces that, in the absence of later glaciation, should be undisturbed. Thirty years ago there was great excitement when a flesher (a tool for scraping skins), made of caribou bone, was found near Old Crow in the northern Yukon and dated to 27,000 BP. But later study showed that it was only about a thousand years old. More recently, caves in the same area have yielded

Gwitch'in winter tent of caribou hide, banked with snow, in a windbreak of trees, drawn by A.H. Murray. Author's collection.

butchered animal bones more than twenty thousand years old, but they are not accompanied by the other human evidence that would clinch the matter.

Conservative archaeologists and anthropologists will not accept a date earlier than the last ice age, and in the absence of indisputable evidence the question must be left open. Everyone agrees, however, that humans had reached the southern tip of the hemisphere by 11,000 BP. This is also the approximate date of the fluted stone points that have been found at widely separated points across the country, the age of which is unquestioned. Northern Canada, the first region to be reached by humans, was also the last to be settled: *Homo sapiens* came to the Yukon at least eleven thousand years ago, but the Inuit did not reach the high Arctic until 2000 BP, and some Inuit populations are even younger than that.

The question of population density in the pre-Columbian Western hemisphere is also controversial. It used to be thought that the population was fairly low, since when Europeans first crossed North America, they encountered wide expanses with no Aboriginal population, or at best a very small one. It also helped to ease the consciences of newcomers to think that the Native population in, say, 1900 was not significantly smaller than it had been in 1500; such an estimate made the process of Europeanization seem less genocidal. Unfortunately for tender consciences, however, this idea is false. The truth seems to be what common sense would suggest: that the population of the Western hemisphere before the Europeans arrived had expanded to the capacity of the land to support it. The debate then becomes one over what this capacity was, which in turn requires an understanding of the indigenous way of life; agriculture as practised east of the Mississippi and in

'Wood figurine of a Dorset man', from *Ancient People of the Arctic* by Robert McGhee. Photograph by Harry Foster. Canadian Museum of Civilization, plate 2: 597-13699.

'Ivory maskette depicting a serene face marked with a complex design that probably represents tattooing', from *Ancient People of the Arctic* by Robert McGhee. Photograph by Harry Foster. Canadian Museum of Civilization, plate 8: 597-13698.

Mark Pitseolak working on a sculpture, Cape Dorset. Fred Bruemmer photo. OF 3216.

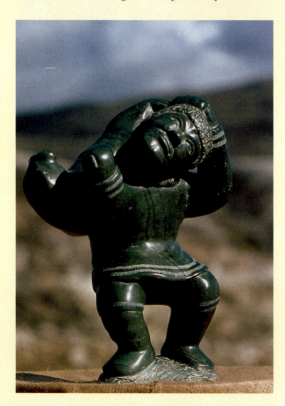

'Man Carrying Seal'. Soapstone carving by Agjagajoo Shaw, Cape Dorset. Fred Bruemmer photo. OF 3314.

Butchering Moose, Lac La
Martre, 1958. NWT Archives,
Ryan Collection., N91-073:0035.

Drying fish and moose, Lac La
Martre, 1958. NWT Archives,
Ryan Collection., N91-073:0017.

Adele Zoe cleaning hide, Lac La
Martre, 1958. NWT Archives,
Ryan Collection., N91-073:0039.

Overnight igloo of a travelling hunter. Fred Bruemmer photo. AX 1615.

Iceberg sculptured by water, off the Labrador coast.
Fred Bruemmer photo. AX 3474.

Central America, for example, could support far more people per square kilometre than could the hunter-gatherer style of northern Canada. Whereas in Central America sophisticated agricultural practices supported a comparatively dense population, in northern Canada the population was perhaps only one per 150 to 250 square kilometres, which means that the pre-contact Yukon might have had a population of five or six thousand. The game and other resources of the region were simply not plentiful enough to support a larger population.

Estimates of the population of what is now Canada and the United States in 1500 run as high as 18 million, though a lower figure, perhaps two or three million, is more probable. For Canada alone the estimates run from 500,000 to two million—again, the lower figure is more generally accepted—of whom perhaps 40 per cent lived on the Pacific coast. What is not disputed, however, is that the mortality of First Nations in the contact period was far higher than anyone would have wanted to admit a century ago. The reason that parts of the continent were 'empty' when the first Europeans explored them was that the First Nations had already been devastated by European diseases that penetrated well ahead of the people who introduced them. As many as nine-tenths of the population of some groups were killed before ever setting eyes on a European; and, with the help of abuses of various kinds in the post-contact period, some groups disappeared entirely—notably the Native people of the Caribbean and some tribes in California.

Although the prehistory of the Western hemisphere involves many hundreds of tribal

A Tanana Indian of the Yukon River Valley, drawn by Frederick Whymper in 1865. Whymper, a Victoria artist, was hired to record the survey of the telegraph route to Siberia, a project that was abandoned when the Atlantic submarine cable was successfully laid. He called his subject 'the ideal North American Indian'. Author's collection.

and linguistic groups living and evolving over many thousands of years, the prehistory of what are now the Yukon and NWT, though complex in its details, concerns only two basic racial and linguistic populations. The two territories are, and seem always to have been, the homeland of two language groups—the Athapaskans (the ancestors of the Dene of the Mackenzie Valley and Yukon) and the Inuit. In other words, almost all the First Nations of the Yukon and NWT belong to the Athapaskan group and speak languages that are closely

Frederick Whymper's depiction of a caribou hunt shows the traditional technique of driving the animals into a 'sur-round' for killing. Author's collection.

related (there are small groups in the southern Yukon of which this is not true). They are descended from people who lived in the same region six or seven thousand years ago. The linguistic history of the Dene suggests that as late as 2700 BP they were a single, closely related people with a homeland in east-central Alaska and the adjacent part of the Yukon. After that date they began to disperse into the regions where they now live, a process that was not completed until about AD 1400. The Inuit of northern Canada also speak a number of different regional dialects of the same language, which they share with the Eskimos of Greenland, Alaska, and Siberia. This general picture is widely accepted, though virtually every detail that makes it up is the subject of scientific controversy, the details of which, as they pertain to the Dene, are summarized for specialists in J.W. Ives's *A Theory of Northern Athapaskan Prehistory* (1990).

It is difficult for the non-specialist to conceive an accurate mental image of what life must have been like for the people who first came to northern Canada. An interesting attempt to draw such a picture has, however, recently been made by the Yukon anthropologist Catharine McClellan. McClellan accepts a date of 25,000 BP for the first human habitation of the Yukon, a date others would dispute,

Fort Yukon, drawn in 1865 by Frederick Whymper, four years before the Americans forced the Hudson's Bay
Company to move it up the Porcupine River into Canada. Author's collection.

but her vignette of life in late winter about 11,000 BP on the Porcupine River seems as accurate a portrait as we are likely to get:

> It is bitterly cold. Although the snow blows about on the arctic tundra, it is rarely deep enough, except for occasional big drifts, to cover the tallest of the stunted willows. . . . Six families are camped in the shelter of some small poplar and spruce that have managed to grow in a sunny, south-facing spot . . . It is hard to keep warm, even though everybody wears shirts and pants made of caribou or elk hide. Some have parkas made of hare pelts which have been cut into strips and woven.

> Each adult has a heavy robe of bison hide too, but only a tiny willow-twig fire burns in the big brush-and-skin shelter . . .

> Suddenly a howl comes from one of the dogs that has been left in camp. Five hunters are approaching, who have been gone for almost a week. Each has on his back a net hunting bag full of dark, rich bison meat. They men have been lucky enough to creep close to a sleeping bison cow, and with their sharp, bone-pointed darts have been able to kill her. Bison meat is rare at this season of the year. . . . The hunters had to follow the herd on foot for many miles before they had a chance to make this kill, but it was a special-

Dene skin tents on Great Slave Lake, early in the twentieth century. NAC, C6975.

ly good one. Butchering the cow, the hunters found an unborn calf in her—just the kind of food to give to the two wise but nearly toothless older men on whose knowledge the welfare of the group depends. . . .

When the meal has ended, the hunters recount just how they got the bison. . . . Finally the oldest man begins a favourite story about a hero whose father-in-law sent him to get the sinews of a giant bison . . . After a while even the adults begin to doze, but two or three listen carefully, one of them silently repeating some of the old man's words. Eleven thousand years later, the story will still be told in the Yukon . . .[2]

The most remarkable part of this picture, from the non-Native point of view, is the suggestion that oral tradition could persist for 11,000 years, and that First Nations society has been sufficiently stable throughout that period to make this possible.

Ten thousand years later, in the spring of AD 1000, the descendants of those people were still there. The land had come to look much the same as it does today, with larger trees and a way of life based on a new animal, the caribou:

> *The men have mended all the birchbark canoes and are ready to launch them at the caribou ford as soon as the animals appear. Men, women and children wait along the bank to drive back into the water any caribou that succeed in crossing the river. A doe appears on the bank, and then another, and another. Soon hundreds of caribou crowd the far shore and more press from behind. After some hesitation, the first arrivals start to swim toward the shore where the people are waiting. When the animals are well out in the river, the men emerge from hiding and launch their canoes into the midst of the swimming herd. They paddle their light craft right up onto the animals' backs. . . . in less than an hour the people have recovered hundreds of carcasses close to the camp, where all can enjoy the fresh meat. Most of the flesh will be dried, to last until summer fishing begins.*[3]

Elderly Dene woman, photographed in 1903. NAC, C5108.

One event that must have dramatically affected these peoples' lives, and can be dated with some accuracy, was a volcanic eruption that took place about 1,250 years ago in the St Elias range, just west of the Alaska–Yukon boundary. This was the White River ash fall, which blew to the east and affected a large part of what is now the Yukon Territory. So much volcanic ash was produced by this eruption—fifteen to thirty cubic kilometres of ejected material—that plants and animals were affected downwind of it for a distance of 1,000 km, and ash fell over an area of 250,000 km². In AD 750 the population of the Yukon was not great, and perhaps only five hundred people were directly affected by this tremendous eruption (vastly greater than the 1980 explosion of Mount St Helens in Washington State), but they were compelled to move south, forcing those in their path to move as well in a kind of falling domino effect. It has been suggested that this eruption eventually led some Athapaskans to move to the southwest of what is now the United States, where they became the ancestors of the modern Navajos and Apaches, two peoples who speak Athapaskan languages. But this theory, like so much else

Dene woman, Fort Good Hope, *c.* 1940. HBC Archives, N7874.

required in a society dominated by modern technology. On this view, the First Nations of northern Canada enjoyed, in the pre-contact period, an amount of leisure time that most Canadian workers today can only dream of. It is an agreeable picture: people unhampered by materialism, owning only what they could carry, and free of the endless acquisitiveness that plagues modern Western society; at liberty to tell stories, dream, or do as they pleased. There were certainly periods of starvation, and life expectancy was shorter than it is today, but this was true even in Western Europe until well into the last century, and it is unlikely that the peoples of the North ever faced a disaster like the Irish potato famine of the 1840s.

The closer one gets to the period of first contact, the more accurate one can be about the Athapaskan peoples. Taking the Yukon River Valley as an example (the customs of those who lived in the Mackenzie region were not greatly different), a good picture can be drawn of their lives. In the late pre-contact period, which for the Yukon was the era around AD 1800, there were six First Nations in the region: the Kutchin (now Gwitch'in), Han, Kaska, Tagish, Tutchone (North and South), and the Teslin or Inland Tlingit, who were not Athapaskans. It would be wrong to think of these groups as petty kingdoms with distinct borders; this is another European concept that does not fit the New World. Rather, they represented, in the words of the anthropologist James VanStone, 'a cultural continuum carried on by a series of interlocking groups whose individual lifeways differed only in minor details from those of their most immediate neighbours'.[5]

Kenneth S. Coates, in *Best Left as Indians*,[6]

concerning the Athapaskans, is the subject of vigorous controversy.

In any case, such theories tell us very little about the people themselves. A view of the northern First Nations that may help to do so was suggested in 1972 by the anthropologist Marshall Sahlins, who asserted that the Athapaskans should be viewed as 'the original affluent society'.[4] Having calculated the amount of work required by these people to obtain food, clothing, fuel, and whatever material goods they needed, Sahlins found it to be only a fraction of the time required by the European peasantry of the Middle Ages to achieve the same goals, or indeed of that a history of the Yukon First Nations in the post-contact period, describes their lives on the eve of penetration of their land by Europeans. These people were hunter-gatherers, or nomads—although to the extent that this term suggests a lack of focus to their lives it is misleading. At particular times of the year they gathered in large groups—during the spring fishing season, for example—but when the fishing was done and the demand for food exceeded the supply, they broke up into smaller groups, based on the extended family, and spread out over the land. The food resources of the North, particularly the large game animals, are not as concentrated as they are farther south, so that the Yukon First Nations needed to hunt over a large area in small groups. In spring and summer they fished, drying some of the catch for later use; in fall and winter they hunted, though in a lean winter the unlucky might starve. All their movements were tied to natural cycles. When the caribou migrated or the salmon came to the rivers to spawn, the people had to be there to intercept them. When the moose had been hunted extensively in one region, the people had to move to another. In many cases they had to travel in search of plants for food and medicine as well.

This sort of mobility necessitated a social structure that to Europeans seemed loose and ill-defined—the antithesis of feudalism or modern systems of industrial organization. The idea of leadership varied according to the task at hand and the skills of individuals: one man might be the hunting leader and another the trading leader. Spiritual leaders, or shamans, had the power to interpret and influence the non-human world. Women lacked formal power, but had great influence as teach-

Dene making birch syrup. NAC, c8952.

ers and story-tellers. The spiritual life of these people, like their material life, did not operate according to a formal code, and was not a 'religion' at all as Europeans understood the word—a fact that led to grave cultural misunderstandings between First Nations and the early missionaries. Rather, their spirituality was practical and functional, a means to bridge the gap between the lives of the people and the lives of animals and the rest of the world. The material and spiritual lives of these people had developed in a continuum stretching back without much interruption for thousands of years. It was not unchanging, but it was a highly developed adaptation to their surroundings. One could argue, without falling into the fallacy of romanticizing the 'noble savage', that these people's lives were in many ways more satisfying than those of the people who were shortly to disrupt them, if for no other reason than that they, unlike the peasants of Europe, were answerable to no one but themselves.

Dog Rib (Dene) tents, Fort Rae, 1914. HBC Archives, N11689.

A glimpse into the lives of these people in the pre-contact period is provided by an account of the annual caribou hunt among the Kutchin (Gwitch'in) people of the northern Yukon. For these people whose lives revolved around the hunting of game, the most important event of the year was the hunt during the fall migration of the Porcupine River caribou herd. Two long rows of wooden sticks would be erected in the path that the people knew from experience the animals would take. The rows of sticks were roughly V-shaped, and served to funnel the animals in an enclosure or 'surround', like a corral, made of branches. Snares made of hide were set, and when the animals followed the path of the sticks, or were stam-

peded into doing so, they became entangled in the snares and could be shot with arrows. Similar techniques included driving the caribou into lakes where they could be speared, and the river-crossing method described above by Catharine McClellan. All these methods produced large quantities of food, some for immediate use and some for storage—unless, as occasionally happened, the migration did not follow its usual path; then the people faced starvation. That the technique of the surround was used until recent times is evident in aerial photographs taken 30 or 40 years ago that show surviving rows of sticks. East of the Mackenzie Mountains, in the Mackenzie River watershed, the Chipewyans also depended on

Arctic Red River, June 1921. HBC Archives, N6314.

the caribou, moving from their homeland north of Lake Athabasca to the Barrenlands in what is now the NWT to follow the herds.

The other indigenous people of northern Canada are the Inuit. Although their first ancestors, like the Dene's, came from Siberia, they arrived much more recently—about 4000 BP—and presumably by boat, since by then the ice age was over and the sea level had risen, submerging Beringia. The Inuit and their ancestors are divided by anthropologists into several 'cultures', according to their way of life, but with one exception they all seem to be biologically and culturally related. The earliest group of migrants to the North were the so-called Palaeo-Eskimos.

Related perhaps to the modern Chukchi of Siberia, they spread from the forests of that part of Russia across the high Arctic to the Greenland coast about 4,000 years ago. Archaeological remains of these people have been found in Greenland and on Ellesmere Island, far to the north of any Inuit settlement in recent centuries. And, most astonishingly, they seem to have lived in skin tents rather than in igloos, keeping themselves warm over fires of twigs, bone, and driftwood. The Danish archaeologist Eigil Knuth has suggested that they passed the long winters in 'a state of torpor'. Robert McGhee has reconstructed what their lives may have been like in the long months of cold and perpetual darkness:

Peter Kaningoak driving Archdeacon Webster's sled, near Holman Island, NWT, 1945. NWT Archives, Learmonth Collection, N87-033:0221.

The return of the hunter wakes up the silent camp. . . . Children tumble out of the tent to slide on the hard snow, while a woman strikes sparks from flint and a small ball of pyrites kept in her sewing kit. Dried moss eventually catches fire, and a tiny flame flickers around the twigs of willow and shavings of driftwood collected with such pains during the previous summer. Then tent is filled with smoke and frozen breath and shadows that jump against the frost crystals condensed on the walls since the last fire. . . . Chunks of meat placed close to the fire begin to thaw; sharp knives quickly shave off the half-frozen food, and it is eaten as soon as human teeth are capable of chew-

ing it. When the fuel runs out, the housewife picks pebbles from the hearth, and drops them hissing into the skin pot packed with snow and scraps of meat. Surprisingly quickly the mixture melts and begins to steam, producing the thin, lukewarm soup that is the main winter sustenance of every family. . . . The smoke hole in the roof is plugged with skins. . . . The families retreat beneath their muskox hide blankets. . . . The camp will sleep for another day, or perhaps until hunger goads them once again to face the waking world.[7]

Hundreds of archaeological sites suggest that this way of life survived in Greenland, and on

Igloo built by Inuit who came to trade at Coppermine, NWT, at Easter 1947. NWT Archives, Osborne Collection, N90-006:0075.

Canada's Ellesmere and Axel Heiberg Islands, for at least 2,000 years, and that different populations of these people lived across the Arctic and as far south as Labrador. The people of this culture spread rapidly from Alaska across the Canadian Arctic coast to Greenland. Like their successors, they lived by hunting seal, caribou, and musk-ox, among other animals. They made fine sharp tools from stone, and are said to have followed the 'Arctic small tool tradition'. Around 2500 BP, in part because of climate changes, they evolved into the Dorset culture, so called because of archaeological finds made at Cape Dorset.

Traces of the Dorset culture dating from about 500 BC to roughly AD 1500 have been found in most coastal regions of Arctic Canada. It was similar in many ways to the culture of the Inuit at the time of contact: the Dorset people had developed the igloo for winter use and turf houses for warm weather; they used dogsleds and kayaks to hunt, and soapstone lamps fuelled by seal oil to light and heat their dwellings. They spread into areas of Canada that modern Inuit do not inhabit— particularly northern Newfoundland, where they lived for more than a thousand years— until they were supplanted or absorbed in their turn by the Thule culture. The Dorset people had a well-developed artistic tradition closely connected to their spiritual beliefs. In fact, it has been suggested that the famous Dorset carvings are evidence of religious tradi-

Drummer, Cape Dorset, NWT, 1967. NWT Archives, Smith Collection, N91-028:0193.

tion and ritual among these people, and that the content of this art is of more importance than its form, reflecting 'the entire social context of thought and action in which the work is embedded'. According to the art historian George Swinton,

> The highly developed and exquisitely shaped objects are not the work of occasional carvers, far less mere whittlers, but the carefully planned and considered work of specialists (either shamans or their helpers), who knew the traditions of form as well as of content, and who applied them in a carefully handed down traditional manner. It is by no means

unreasonable to conceive of a Dorset artist-shaman (or a shaman artist) as the main producer of such art.[8]

The modern Inuit have an oral tradition of the Dorset people that is reinforced by the remains of their culture that still exist. As Peter Pitseolak, a well-known Inuit photographer who died in 1973, recalled:

> In the Cape Dorset area there are many graves of the Tooniks—the early people. They are usually by the shore—they're all over the place if you really look. The Tooniks were very short and very strong people and their graves

*were shorter than ordinary Eskimo graves. . . .
They covered them over with stones. . . . The
Tooniks lived in giant houses that were made
of stone. . . .We used to see them when we
were passing by. You could even see the doors.
Up to today if you touch the stones you still
get soot on your fingers.*[9]

The Thule culture was a later development
of the Inuit way of life, coming from Alaska
about AD 1000 and surviving until about 1600,
though it is thought that the culture of the
Sadlermuit—the Inuit of Southampton Island
in Hudson Bay, who died out at the beginning
of this century—was a remnant of the Thule
culture. The Thule people perfected the techniques of hunting on the open sea, and were
able to take even such large sea mammals as
the bowhead whale. Living in permanent vil-
lages in houses constructed of turf, stone, and
whalebone, they used metal knives and tools
that they either made from local deposits, such
as the native copper found at the Coppermine
River, or obtained through trade with the
Norse in Greenland. Although their economy
and culture deteriorated after 1600, when the
climate cooled, they are the direct ancestors of
the modern Inuit.

There are memories of the Thule culture
that date almost to the present. Peter Pitseolak
recounted the stories of a man, a friend of his
father, who visited Southampton Island on a
whaling ship before the turn of the century. It
had apparently been some years since any
other Inuit had made contact with them:

*I heard from Kingwatsiak these people were
talking like small babies, unable to pronounce
correctly. And they were very, very messy with*

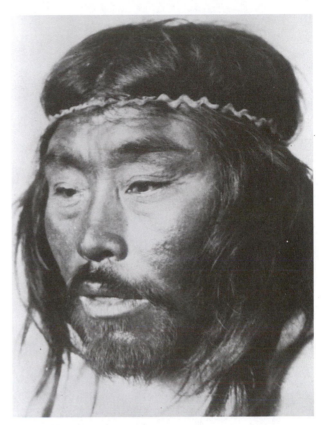

Angakok (shaman), Eskimo Point, NWT, *c.* 1935. NWT
Archives, Fleming Collection, N79-050:0646.

*their animal flesh. The didn't clean them-
selves. We called them the 'Pujite', which
means 'dried-up oil.' All the oil and blubber
was caked into them. . . . Years before, people
from our side used to go across to
Southampton Island in their skin boats using
the inukshuks [cairns of stone in human
shape] at Inukshuk Point as guides. At that
time people from our side called the Pujite,
'Takoogatarak,' meaning 'we are shy with
them', because even before the skin boats go to
shore the men there would try to trade wives
with them. Then they'd say in their baby voices, 'They don't want it, they don't want it.' . . .*

Hunting white whale, Western Arctic, 1936. HBC Archives, N7224.

After the Southampton Island people died off and there was no one there, the people from this side started to move there.[10]

The culture of the modern Inuit has developed over the past five centuries, but it is based on older Inuit cultures that go back four thousand years. The details of this culture are well known, since it existed with very little change well into the present century, and important parts of it still exist, unaffected by the disruptions to which the people have been subjected. The basic Inuit social group was

and is composed of two or three families, usually related, operating as a social and economic unit. Such a group functioned as a large extended family, sharing hunting responsibilities, child-raising, and other tasks. Because the harsh environment made it difficult for anyone to survive alone, sharing, or social cooperation, was a central feature of Inuit culture. The most prized personality traits were friendliness and good humour—the proper response to misfortune was laughter—and a person who displayed bad temper or unfriendliness might be ostracized or killed as a potential danger to the extended family unit. More than one violent or surly newcomer found this out to his cost.

The economy of almost all the Inuit was based on sea-dwelling mammals, notably seals, walrus, and bowhead whales, although birds, fish, and smaller game also made up part of their diet, according to the season. With tremendous ingenuity the Inuit made use of whatever came to hand. They used every part of the animals they killed—the sinews (string and rope), bladders (floats and containers), and intestines (sails for kayaks), as well as the meat, fur, bones, and skin. Their caribou-skin clothes gave much better protection against the Arctic cold than anything available to Europeans before the middle of the twentieth century. And, without trees for building, they made houses out of snow, with windows of clear lake ice. These were the people who would clash with the Norse in AD 1000, and with Martin Frobisher six hundred years later.

Inukshuit (*inukshuk* means 'in the form of a person'; *inukshuit* is the plural), Cape Dorset, NWT, 1968. NWT Archives, Smith Collection, N91-028:0036.

CHAPTER THREE

Newcomers

*I*n 1992 a remarkable non-event took place in North America: the five-hundredth anniversary of the arrival of Christopher Columbus in the Western hemisphere was not celebrated. What was remarkable was the embarrassed silence with which this anniversary was greeted. Had it occurred fifty years ago, it would have been marked with parades, fireworks, the unveiling of statues, the renaming of streets, and all the other honours with which our society worships its heroes. But in 1992 the occasion was noted in Canada and the United States by some half-hearted attempts at celebration on the part of citizens of Italian descent, a movie or two that died at the box office, and, above all, denunciations of Columbus as a representative of the forces of European imperialism. In our age Columbus is no longer the hero-explorer; he is the bringer of disease, degradation, and death to millions of Native Americans, the harbinger of genocide. This is quite a recent view; as late as 1974, in Samuel Eliot Morison's superb account of the European discovery (he uses the word without quotation marks) of North America,[1] the death of virtually the entire

indigenous population of the Caribbean is treated in a matter-of-fact fashion, and Columbus and his men are portrayed as rather a jolly crew. Today we are less comfortable with a man who reported to his royal masters that the Native people were entirely tractable and would make fine slaves. Thus historical fashions change.

Columbus never went near the Canadian North, but the reputations of those 'discoverers' who did, though none are as famous as he, have gradually waned with changing attitudes. Nor was he even the first European to see the Americas. The Canadian North was visited by Europeans half a millennium before Columbus brought wealth to Spain and death to the West Indies. The question of which person from the Old World was the first to visit the New is one of the 'mysteries' of history that tend to attract cranks as well as scholars, and perhaps more of the former than the latter. The desire to undercut Columbus's primacy in the field was explained thus by the famous naturalist and traveller Alexander von Humboldt (1769–1859): 'There are three stages in the popular attitude toward a great discovery: first, men doubt its existence, next they deny its importance, and finally they give the credit to someone else.' Ethnic pride is also an important factor. The list of putative pre-Columbian discoverers of the New World includes St Brendan the Navigator (born *c.* 484), the Irish monk whose voyages to unknown lands in the Atlantic Ocean are recorded in *Navigatio Sancti Brendani Abbatis,* manuscripts of which date to the tenth century; Prince Madoc of Wales, who came to America in the late twelfth century and taught the Mandans of North Dakota to speak Welsh; the Zeno brothers of Venice in the fourteenth century; Pining and Pothorst, Saxon pirates; Johannes Scolvus, a Pole; and many, many others. Hardly any national group lacks a claimant; recently an African-American scholar put forward the claim that African explorers reached the New World long before any European. There is no evidence whatever for any of these prior expeditions, but the stories refuse to die. They are kept alive by people, many of them autodidacts, who write books full of phrases such as 'it is entirely possible that' and 'might well have', and who resent the scorn with which academics greet them. The 'unexplained' pre-Columbian artefacts they point to as evidence of exploration invariably have a better explanation—if they are not outright frauds.

The Canadian North, however, was the site not only of pre-Columbian exploration but of actual settlement, the reality of which is now beyond serious question. The explorers were the Norsemen, and their story, told in two Icelandic sagas dating from the thirteen century, has been confirmed (unlike the tales of St Brendan and the others) by archaeological evidence. An important difference between

Sir Martin Frobisher, who spent three summers (1576–78) looking for gold in the bay that now bears his name. NAC, C11413.

the voyage of Leif Ericsson (d. *c.* 1020), who reached Baffin Island in the summer of 1001, and the supposed voyages of St Brendan and the others was that Ericsson's voyage was not a tremendous leap into the unknown, as voyages by the Irish, or the Egyptians, or the Gambians, or any of the others would have been, but a fairly simple progression in a series of steps that had already been taken. For Ericsson came from Greenland, where his father, Eric the Red, had set up a settlement in 985 with a number of people from Iceland, a country that had in turn been colonized by Norwegians. Apparently he was not even the first of his people to see what is now Canada: Bjarni Herjolfsson had sighted Labrador fifteen years before him.

In the summer of 1001, Ericsson and a crew of thirty-five sailed in a *knarr* (a tubbier vessel than the better-known Viking long ship) in search of good timber, which Greenland lacked. He made land at Baffin Island, which he called 'Helluland', the country of flat stones; but, finding nothing there of value to him, he did not stay. He put in again at 'Markland', or land of forests, which was 'level and wooded, with broad white beaches . . . and a gently sloping shoreline'; this S.E. Morison identifies as the coast of Labrador at 54° north. Again sailing south, he came to

> *a place where a stream flows out of a lake, where they cast anchor [after which] they took their leather sleeping bags ashore and built themselves shelters. Later they decided to stay there during the winter and set up large houses. There was no lack of salmon either in the river or the lake, and it was bigger salmon than they had ever seen. Nature was so generous here that it seemed to them no cattle would need any winter fodder, but could graze outdoors. . . . The days and nights were more nearly equal than in Greenland or Iceland. On the shortest day of winter the sun was up between breakfast time and late afternoon.*[2]

This was 'Vinland', the location of which has been debated for centuries. In the early 1960s the archaeologist Helge Ingstad began work at L'Anse aux Meadows, on the northern tip of Newfoundland, a site that he identified with Vinland. There was at first much skepticism about this claim, but the unearthing of house foundations in the Norse style provided powerful evidence, which was clinched by the discovery of Norse artefacts, including a spinning whorl. If L'Anse aux Meadows was not Vinland, it was a Norse settlement of the same period, and it has an excellent claim to the title of the oldest European settlement in the Western hemisphere. The settlement lasted only a year, though it was briefly reoccupied in 1013. There were few volunteers for the colony, and relations with the Inuit (whom the Norse called 'Skraelings', or stunted people) were marked by treachery and violence on both sides. Greenlanders travelled to North America in search of timber for at least three hundred years more (the last recorded voyage was in 1347), but there were no more settlements, and by the middle of the next century even the Greenland colony had died out. Although only 145 years passed between the last Norse voyage and that of Columbus, the Italian explorer apparently knew nothing about the earlier European exploration of North America; and in any case timber was not what he was seeking. Vinland and even Greenland were forgotten by the rest of Europe, and when a Portuguese captain came upon the southern tip of that island in 1500, he mapped it as a new discovery.

Europeans sailed again to what is now Canada quite soon after Columbus reached the Caribbean (and perhaps even before; some historians believe that Basque fishermen were active in the Grand Banks before 1492). In the summer of 1497 John Cabot, a Genoese living in Bristol, reached and claimed Newfoundland for the British. Although it is quite likely that Basque fishermen had visited Baffin Island earlier in the sixteenth century, the first explorer to

HMS *Assistance* and *Pioneer* in winter quarters, 1853. The ships have been prepared for the Arctic winter, with decks roofed over for warmth, and hulls reinforced and insulated with blocks of snow. NAC, C41305.

make an important voyage to what is now the Northwest Territories was Martin Frobisher (1539–94), a professional mariner from Yorkshire. One of the hard, driving men who helped to make Elizabethan England an important force in world affairs, in his teens he had gone on two expeditions to West Africa, and in his early twenties he had served in one of the many unsuccessful English attempts to subjugate Ireland. He made his living as a trader and a part-time privateer, and was three times arrested on charges of piracy, though, like others who were wise enough to give a percentage to the Queen, he was never convicted.

Frobisher came to the Canadian North in 1576 as the first in a long line of his countrymen who would search for the Northwest Passage. This quest, originally motivated by the desire for trade with Asia, and in time simply by national pride, would continue for more than three hundred years; beginning with the Elizabethans, it was not accomplished until the first years of this century, by which time it had long lost any commercial importance. In Frobisher's day, however, it promised fortunes in spices and silks, and Frobisher's reputation as a captain made it easy for him to raise fifteen hundred pounds to build a ship of

Group of Inuit, *c.* 1823; etching by George F. Lyon (1795–1832). NAC, C25703.

twenty tonnes, the *Gabriell*; to buy another somewhat larger one, the *Michaell*; and to hire a crew of thirty-five.

On 7 June 1576 Queen Elizabeth waved goodbye as the ships passed Greenwich, and on 28 July they reached the southern tip of Baffin Island. Sailing north, they entered the great bay that still bears Frobisher's name; he thought it was 'a great gutte, bay, or passage' separating Asia from North America, and named it after himself. It was, he said, 'Frobishers Streytes, lyke as Magellanus at the Southwest ende of the Worlde, having discovered the passage to the South Sea, called the same straites Magellanes streightes.' He sailed deep into the bay and went ashore to be greeted by the Inuit, who traded furs and meat for European clothing. Frobisher described them thus: 'They be like to Tartars, with long blacke haire, broad faces, and flatte noses, and tawnie in colour, wearing Seale skinnes . . . the women are marked in the face with blewe streakes down the cheekes, and round about the eies.' The Inuit (Frobisher called them 'the savages' or 'the country people') seemed friendly, but when five of his men, against orders, rowed out of sight in a small boat to do some trading on their own, they disappeared and were never seen again.

Frobisher and his crew returned to England with two prizes. One was an Inuk captured, with his kayak, just before their departure. According to Michael Lok, the director of the Muscovy company and one of Frobisher's backers, the 'strange man and his bote, which was such a wonder unto the city and to the rest of the realm' was a great curiosity in London, but he soon caught a cold and died. The collection of Native people as if they were botanical specimens was quite common in that era; no thought at all was given to their wishes, and once in Europe they invariably died in short order of some common disease to which they had no immunity.

The other prize was a piece of rock containing glittering specks. Lok took the rock to three different assayers, all of whom said it was iron pyrite, commonly known as 'fool's gold'. A fourth assayer was found, however, who discovered what he claimed were traces of real gold in it; when Lok asked him how he had found what others had missed, he replied that it was sometimes necessary 'to know how to flatter nature'. There was indeed plenty of gold in the Canadian North, but none of it lay anywhere near Frobisher Bay, and when it was discovered, three hundred years later, it turned out to be on the other side of the continent, in the Yukon. This kind of delusion was an example of what the French called *diamants du Canada*, 'Canadian diamonds', a scornful phrase describing something phony, after Cartier's claim that he had found diamonds on his voyage of 1535. It was just as well for the Inuit that Frobisher's rocks were fool's gold; had the gold been real, it would have attracted the cupidity of the English, and the indigenous people of Baffin Island would likely have suffered the same fate as those of Hispaniola.

The rocks nevertheless aroused the interest of backers, and in 1577 a second expedition set sail for Baffin Island. This was a grander affair than the first one, consisting of three ships and 120 men; Queen Elizabeth contributed a thousand pounds and one of the ships. Having survived a voyage through 'monstrous and huge yce, comparable to great mountains', the crew spent the summer in Frobisher Bay, returning to England with 200 tonnes of ore and three Inuit—a man, a woman, and a child, all of whom soon died. On this trip Frobisher searched for the crew members who had disappeared the previous summer, but no trace of them was found. Their fate was discovered nearly three hundred years later, when the American explorer Charles Francis Hall visited the region in 1862. According to the local oral tradition, the Inuit had not killed the five men but kept them captives until after Frobisher's third and final expedition, when they let them go. The five men had scrounged sufficient timber from the expedition's remains to build a small boat in which they set sail for England, but they were lost at sea. The story was testimony to the remarkable strength of oral history among the Inuit.

The English investors found assayers who told them that the 200 tonnes of iron pyrite contained gold enough to show a profit on the voyage. Thus encouraged, in 1578 they sent a third, even larger expedition to Baffin Island. This one had fifteen ships and cost six thousand pounds; most of the investors were members of the nobility, and the Queen herself put up half the money. The earlier trips had been fairly easy, but this time Frobisher was blown off course and became the first European to see Hudson Strait (which he called the 'Mistaken Straites'), up which he sailed a considerable distance before realizing where he was and turning back. The crew spent the summer mining on Kodlunarn Island, where the trenches they dug can still be seen, along with traces of a stone house built for an experiment in wintering-over (cancelled when Frobisher changed his mind). They returned to London with 2,000 tonnes of ore. Smelters tried for five years to extract gold from it, but eventually the truth had to be admitted: the ore was worthless. A large fortune had been wasted and the company broke up amidst mutual recriminations. Going on to fight alongside Drake in the West Indies, Frobisher died of wounds in 1594.

Frobisher's voyages set the pattern for expeditions to northern Canada for the next two hundred years, the age in which it was hoped that Arctic exploration would bring wealth (it would be followed by another century in which the chief goal was glory). Sailing in total ignorance of where he was going or what he was likely to find, with wildly unrealistic expectations of the rewards, disappointing the investors who backed him, and failing in his primary task of finding the Northwest Passage, Frobisher nevertheless put an important part of Canada on the maps of Europe.

It would be wrong to think of the era of the search for wealth and the Northwest Passage as one of continuous progress, in which each explorer penetrated farther north and west, and was more successful in his search, than his predecessor. From the sixteenth century to the eighteenth, more depended on skill and luck than on precedent.

Some of the early voyages, for instance, were remarkably successful. An example is John Davis (*c.* 1550–1605), another Elizabethan mariner, who made three voyages in search of the passage, in 1585, 1586, and 1587. On the third he had the good fortune to encounter an ice-free season, and reached a latitude of 72°46' on the Greenland coast. He gave his name to the Davis Strait and to Davis Inlet in Labrador. Four years later, exploring in a quite different direction, he discovered (here the word is apt, since they were unoccupied) the Falkland Islands.

An even more remarkable voyage for that period was that of Thomas Baffin (*c.* 1584–1622), probably the most proficient Arctic navigator of his time, who in 1616, in the course of yet another search for the Northwest Passage, sailed 500 kilometres farther north than Davis had, to 77°45', a record that stood for 236 years. On an earlier voyage Baffin had explored the west end of Hudson Strait, which he reported did not lead to the Northwest Passage; had mapped much of the coast of the island that bears his name; and had calculated through astronomical observations the first accurate longitude ever obtained at sea.

These explorers and their contemporaries—Waymouth, Knight, James, Munk, Bylot, Button, and the rest—left hardly a trace on the land (only some rock cuttings in Frobisher Bay) but a persistent memory in the minds of the Native people. Most of their activity consisted of sailing in and out of bays and inlets, mapping, some desultory trading with the Inuit, and in general managing to stay alive—no mean feat, given the conditions and the resources at their disposal. Perhaps their most important achievement was to bring the

Canadian North to the attention of Europe. Much of the exploratory activity that was later to prove important to the region came about by accident, as in the case of Henry Hudson (*fl.* 1607–11). Hudson, like the rest, was looking for the Northwest Passage, and in the course of his search became the first European to enter Hudson Bay. Wintering at the mouth of the Rupert River, he was unable to manage his mutinous crew; they set him adrift the next summer and he vanished without trace. But his skills, unfortunately not equalled by his capacities as a leader, had opened a huge inland sea and a short route to the interior of the continent. Hundreds would soon follow in his wake.

CHAPTER FOUR

Fur Traders
and Missionaries

*T*he story of the fur trade is in many ways the early story of Canada itself. The same is true of northern Canada, where much of the impetus for exploration and contact with Native people, and the region's economy, revolved for many years around the fur trade. That trade came late to the North, however, in the latter half of the eighteenth century—more than two hundred years after Europeans fishing the Grand Banks first realized there was money to be made in trading cloth and metal goods for beaver pelts.

In 1670 Charles II of England gave a charter to the Hudson's Bay Company, granting it a monopoly in trade in the entire watershed of Hudson Bay; known as Rupert's Land, this area included part of the modern Northwest Territories. For a century after the charter was granted, however, the company adopted a passive policy towards trade. Posts were built at the mouths of major rivers flowing into Hudson Bay and James Bay—at York Factory (1684), Churchill, where Fort Prince of Wales, an impressive stone structure, was begun in 1717, Fort Albany (1684), and other places. Yet the company did not use these forts as

bases for expansion into the interior; rather, it expected the Indians to travel down the rivers to the coast in order to trade. With only one exception—a small post inland on the Albany River—this remained the company's policy for a hundred years. It worked well enough so long as the HBC's main competitors, the French fur traders operating from Montreal, presented no challenge in the interior of the continent; but after the British conquest of Quebec, in 1759, changes had to be made.

Following the formal transfer of Quebec to Britain, in 1763, a group of English and Scottish entrepreneurs took over the old French trade, which had already made tentative forays into the Canadian prairies under Pierre Gaultier de Varennes et de La Vérendrye (1685–1749) and his sons in the 1730s and 1740s. As we shall see, the newly aggressive Montreal traders pushed northwest from the prairies into the Athabasca country, the southern part of the Arctic watershed, forcing the Hudson's Bay Company to respond by sending expeditions into the interior and founding new posts far from the ocean. When, in the 1780s, the Montreal traders coalesced into the North

West Company, they constituted a trading force that was for a while unbeatable.

It was the North West Company that first carried the fur trade north of the 60th parallel into the modern Northwest Territories. Alexander Mackenzie's exploration of the river that bears his name, discussed in the next chapter, was quickly followed by an extension of trade. The North West Company built Fort of the Forks (later renamed Fort Simpson) just after 1800, and Fort Good Hope, the first post on the lower Mackenzie, in 1805. The logistics of transporting trade goods from Montreal to Fort Good Hope and returning with furs will stagger the imagination of anyone who locates the place on a map. Goods were taken by large canoe from Montreal to Fort William at the head of Lake Superior. There they were transferred into smaller canoes for the journey to Lake Winnipeg, up that lake into the North Saskatchewan River, across Methye Portage into the Athabasca, down that river into Lake Athabasca, down the Slave River into Great Slave Lake (Mackenzie's route), and down the Mackenzie to Fort Good Hope. The trip took two years each way, and the average time from the day that a copper kettle left the company's warehouse in London until the beaver pelt that paid for it arrived was an astonishing seven years. The feat was analogous to trading with Mars. In fact, it was in part the tremendous overhead costs of doing business in this way that eventually defeated the North West Company and in 1821 forced it to merge with its older rival.

After the merger, the newly revitalized Hudson's Bay Company extended its operations throughout the Mackenzie Valley as far as Fort McPherson, which was founded in 1840 as Peel's River Post. From this base the HBC

A fortune in furs collected by Revillon Frères, location unknown, winter 1914–15. NWT Archives, Learmonth Collection, N87-033:0061.

began in the 1840s to expand over the Mackenzie Mountains into the Yukon River Valley. By now the economics of the fur trade were changing. The market for beaver pelts, which had been the mainstay of the trade since it began in Canada, had declined in the previous decade as felt hats, made from beaver fur, fell out of favour and were replaced by more fashionable silk hats. As a result, the emphasis shifted to luxury furs, to be worn for warmth and style, and the animals in demand now were fox, mink, and marten. The Yukon River basin was particularly rich in the latter.

Fort Yukon, *c.* 1895, with the North American Trading and Transportation store in the centre of the photo. Author's collection.

The western boundary of what is now the Canadian North was drawn up by the Russians and the British by treaty in 1825. The Russians had been active in coastal Alaska since the middle of the previous century, and laid claim to a large but vaguely defined part of northwestern North America. The British also claimed much of the continent. But the interests of the two countries were not in true conflict. What the Russians really wanted was to be able to trade along the Pacific coast for sea otter and other furs, while the British wanted a monopoly in the interior for the Hudson's Bay Company. The treaty satisfied both desires: a strip of land later called the 'panhandle',

extending south along the coast to latitude 54°40', was reserved for the Russians. The 141st meridian was rather arbitrarily selected, running north from the 60th parallel, as the line east of which the British would operate a monopoly. No one knew then that a treasure-trove of gold lay just east of the line, or that at the end of the century the lack of precision in defining the panhandle would cause an international incident. For the present, the treaty worked well.

Although no fur traders visited the indigenous people of the Yukon before 1840, trade goods had circulated there for many years, brought by Native middlemen from the

The Hudson's Bay Co. trading steamer *Distributor* on the Mackenzie River, sometime in the 1920s. HBC Archives, N6770.

Russians on the Alaskan coast, and later from the traders in the Mackenzie Valley. Indeed, early attempts to found posts in the Yukon were foiled by the people of the Peel River region, who profited from this secondary trade. The Yukon First Nations, on the other hand, were anxious to be visited by traders, and travelled to Peel's River Post to urge the HBC to come and trade with them. The task of opening the trade was given to John Bell, but his early attempts were frustrated by the middlemen, who told him tall tales of the difficulty of the trip over the mountains to the Yukon, and when he persisted in going, led him partway there and then abandoned him. Even-

tually, in 1845, Bell hired Native guides who were not involved in the trade, and was able to reach the 'Youcon' river. In 1846 Lapierre's House was set up on the west side of the mountains, and in 1847 Alexander Hunter Murray led a party to the junction of the Yukon and Porcupine Rivers, where they built Fort Youcon. This site was in Alaska, out of the jurisdiction of the HBC, but it was so remote—over 1,100 kilometres upstream from Nulato, the nearest Russian post—that the Russians took no notice of it.

The second thrust into the Yukon came from the south, from what is now northern British Columbia. In 1839–40 Robert Camp-

Inuit arriving to trade at Repulse Bay, c. 1920. HBC Archives, N8393.

bell established posts on the upper Pelly River and Frances Lake for the Hudson's Bay Company, but his attempt to push farther into the Yukon was frustrated for several years by the Native middlemen, who feared they would be put out of business. In 1848 he succeeded in establishing Fort Selkirk at the junction of the Yukon and Pelly Rivers. However, he found that he had intruded into a well-established trading network, in which the Tlingit from the coast had come inland for years to trade with the Yukon First Nations. They naturally resented the competition, and in the summer of 1852 a group of them burned Fort

Selkirk to the ground as Campbell watched helplessly. Discouraged, the company abandoned the site and concentrated on the trade down river at Fort Yukon.

Students of the fur trade in Canada have long debated the degree to which the First Nations controlled it. To put the question in its extreme form, were they exploited victims of European capitalism, or did they shape the trade to suit their own needs? The history of the nineteenth-century trade in the Yukon provides good evidence for the latter interpretation. The Youcon First Nations, for instance, simply refused to accept the trading terms

Employees of the Hudson's Bay Co. at Eskimo Point, NWT, 1926. NWT Archives, Learmonth Collection, N87-033:0209.

offered by the Hudson's Bay Company in their entirety. The most desirable trade goods were rifles, which made hunting much easier and more productive, and beads, which were a mainstay of an important aspect of the people's art—the decoration of clothing. The company, knowing this, tried to insist that guns and beads could be traded only for the high-value furs, white fox and marten. But the Native peoples refused to trade at all unless all their pelts, beaver as well as the more valuable skins, were accepted in exchange for these goods.

Even more interesting is the psychological warfare waged by the Yukon First Nations on the Hudson's Bay Company at Fort Youcon. The post was weak and vulnerable, a tremendous distance from headquarters over a long and difficult supply route, and moreover was operating illegally in Russian territory. The Native people knew this. Not only were they willing to travel the long distance to trade with the Russians in order to defy the HBC, but they told the company's men at Fort Youcon that the Russians had put a cannon on a boat and were planning to sail up river to throw the intruders out. This was not true, as the company eventually discovered, but the threat did succeed in extracting better terms. A more

Dene using a fur press to prepare furs for shipment, Fort Rae, NWT. NAC, c16441.

ominous threat, offered from time to time, was to attack Fort Youcon and destroy it as Fort Selkirk had been destroyed. In this early period the First Nations and the Hudson's Bay Company existed in a state of uneasy equilibrium, for the company could make no profit without Native co-operation, and would have been helpless against another attack. The First Nations, for their part, wanted and increasingly needed the European trade goods; not only were the Russians a long way off, but their trade goods were inferior.

This situation persisted until the United States purchased Alaska in 1867. Unlike the Russians, the Americans objected to the presence of an HBC post on their territory, and in

1869 Captain Charles Raymond of the US Navy was sent up the Yukon River to tell them to leave. As a result the company moved its post upstream to Rampart House, where it remained until 1890, when a more accurate survey showed that it was still slightly west of the 141st meridian; again it was moved, and in the 1920s it would relocate once more, to Old Crow. American traders, particularly the Alaska Commercial Company, made their way into the interior of Alaska and later into the Yukon, providing the Native people with a real alternative to the Hudson's Bay Company, one they were quick to exploit.

The fur trade in the Yukon and Northwest Territories altered very little during the rest of

Paulette Annegolok (left) and Anne Webster modelling furs at the Hudson's Bay Post at Coppermine, 1943. NWT Archives, Learmonth Collection, N87-033:0512.

the 1800s. At the very end of the century, however, for the first time since the demise of the North West Company, the Hudson's Bay Company faced organized competition from a rival firm. This was Revillon Frères, a Paris fashion house that, tired of buying from the HBC, had decided to trade directly for its furs. Arriving in Edmonton in 1899, Revillon soon built posts in the Northwest Territories, the Athabasca country, and the far north of Quebec, and other firms were formed in Edmonton to trade in the Mackenzie Valley. The result was the same as it had been a century earlier, when the HBC was locked in its struggle with the North West Company. The competition for furs led the traders to encourage over-hunting and -trapping, resulting in quick depletion of local resources and ensuing hardship for the Native people.

This rivalry was carried into the most remote parts of the inhabited North after the beginning of the twentieth century, as fur posts were opened at Chesterfield Inlet on Hudson Bay, Ennadai Lake in the Barrens, and other places such as Coppermine and Tree River along the Arctic coast, as well as Pangnirtung and Lake Harbour on Baffin Island. The goal was to bring the Inuit for the first time into an organized fur economy, trading white fox skins for manufactured goods. Inuit middlemen

The Rev. Thomas Oomak, the first Inuk to be ordained by the Anglican Church, *c.* 1934. NWT Archives, Fleming Collection, N79-050:0085.

were used to carry the trade to isolated groups in areas far from the posts, and by 1920 there were few if any Inuit who were not in contact with these posts, if only at second hand. At the height of the white fox trade, in the late 1920s, there were some ninety posts in the Yukon and Northwest Territories.

The effects of the fur trade on the Indian peoples of northern Canada have been debated, but the effects on the Inuit were quite different, and not so controversial. The Inuit as a people had, or at least were perceived by non-Natives as having, a different attitude towards trade and property than the other indigenous peoples.

They seemed to have an inborn commercial instinct that was not unlike that of the newcomers. They disliked going into debt, and when they did they paid their loans back on time; they could not be fobbed off with trinkets; and (perhaps surprisingly for a culture that had always travelled light) they had no objection to the accumulation of wealth and property. When the North-West Mounted Police first encountered the Inuit in the early years of this century, they were delighted to find them friendly, co-operative, thrifty, and acquisitive—in contrast to the Dene, of whom they had a lower opinion. Inspector A.M. Jarvis of the

'The Prince of Wales Striking Against the Rocks on the East Side of Resolution Island, Hudson Strait', painted in 1819 by Robert Hood (1797–1821), a member of Franklin's first expedition. Hood was murdered in the Barrenlands by a member of his party. NAC, C40321.

'Ervick, a Native of Prince Regents Bay', painted in 1819 by John Ross (1777–1856). NAC, C100068.

'A Canoe of [Franklin's] Northern Land Expedition Chasing Reindeer in Little Martin Lake, NWT', 1820. Watercolour by Robert Hood. NAC, C40360.

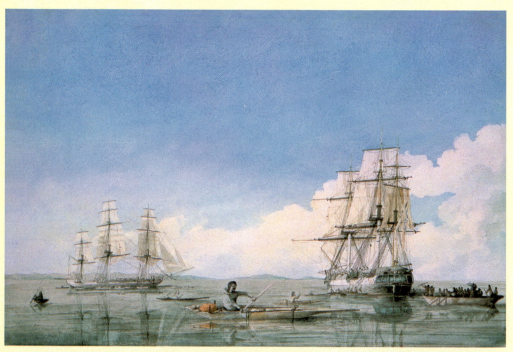

The Hudson's Bay Company ships *Prince of Wales* and *Eddystone* bartering with Inuit off the Upper Savage Islands, Hudson Strait, 1819. Watercolour by Robert Hood. NAC C40364.

Washing for lunch outside the school at Lac La Martre, 1958. NWT Archives, Ryan Collection, N91-073:0059.

Cemetery Day, Lac La Martre, 1958. NWT Archives, Ryan Collection, N91-073:0051.

Fr. Pochat and congregation blessing cross, Lac La Martre, 1958. NWT Archives, Ryan Collection, N91-073:0050.

A man teaches his son to spot caribou with a telescope. Fred Bruemmer photo. AX 2238.

Deacon Amos Njootli and the Rev. T.H. Canham with a wedding party at New Rampart House, Yukon, *c.* 1915. Author's collection.

NWMP, speaking of the Inuit of the Mackenzie Delta region in 1908, commented:

> one need only go 100 miles down the Mackenzie River, and he will find the men either out trapping, or fishing through the ice. The women are either making skin boots or clothing, or smoking cigaretts [sic] or laughing. . . . They are not improvident like the Indians. They very seldom take debt, [but if they do] . . . the first thing they do is to come in with the furs to pay what they owe.[1]

By 1930 the Hudson's Bay Company traders reported that the Inuit were trading their furs for flour, sugar, butter, and canned food at the posts, and that those who had made money trapping white fox had bought gramophones, cameras, and sewing machines, as well as high-powered rifles and outboard motors. The fur trade declined dramatically in the 1930s, however, as the market for luxuries dried up. The prices paid for white fox dropped 80 per cent between 1929 and 1935, putting independent traders out of business, forcing many of the posts to close, and in some cases causing severe hardship for the people who, in the space of just a few years, had come to depend

A romanticized view of the clergy in the Yukon: Bishop W.C. Bompas and a Native companion working towards a common goal. Anglican Church Archives, P7517-204.

on them; when the post at Ennadai Lake closed at the end of the Second World War, the Inuit of the region were reduced to starvation and death. In later decades the fur trade would be seriously damaged by the protests of Greenpeace and other environmental movements, and would decline as a staple of northern income, particularly in relation to the growing importance of government transfer payments, but it is still an important part of the cash income of many indigenous people in the North.

The other great outside force working upon the Native people of the North in this period was religion. No subject in the long history of the relations between the First Nations in Canada and the newcomers is more controversial than the effects of the missionaries and churches upon them and their culture, and this is as true in the North as in the rest of the country. Of all the activities of European society, missionary work is perhaps the most difficult for many members of today's secular society to understand, let alone to sympathize with. Everyone knows what the Hudson's Bay Company had to gain in pushing into the Mackenzie Valley, for instance; the profit motive is comprehensible even to those who disapprove of it. But what were the missionaries there for? To appreciate the answer we must understand that the Victorian era was a high point of Protestant evangelicalism, in which generally well-meaning and often devout people endeavoured to spread the Christian gospel over large stretches of the world—to Asia, Africa, and Australia in particular. At the same time the Roman Catholic Church was anxious to spread its version of the gospel wherever it could. The Bible made it clear that spreading the good news was a duty for Christians, and in the great age of imperial expansion, it was easy for missionaries to go where the army and the traders had gone—or sometimes to go before them.

It might seem that northern Canada, cold, remote, and inaccessible, would have been a field eagerly sought by missionaries as a place where Christian endeavour and physical hardship would find approval in the sight of God. But this was not always the case. Most Protestant missionaries preferred to go to Africa and Asia, where millions of souls waited

Roman Catholic Mission, Arctic Bay, NWT, 1970. NWT Archives, Smith Collection, N91-028:0214.

to be saved. Northern Canada, with its comparative handful of potential converts, was a distinct third choice, and did not attract the most brilliant graduates of the theological schools. The Roman Catholic Church, on the other hand, sent its best and brightest recruits to the most difficult and inhospitable places.

Because the Canadian North was not really opened to trade until the middle of the nineteenth century, well-organized missionary efforts were ready to penetrate the region as soon as it was possible to do so; the Church Missionary Society of the Church of England and the Roman Catholics were on the starting line almost simultaneously. Beginning around 1850, Anglicans and Catholics engaged in a hot rivalry, a race for souls, that would continue for many decades. Each side enjoyed some advantages over the other. The Hudson's Bay Company, which controlled the trade and the transportation network of the North, was at first ambivalent about the presence of any missionaries in its territory; religion was good for Native people to the extent that it 'civilized' them, but the missionaries were forever trying to get the them to settle down and become more domestic, which was not good for trade. Eventually, when the company recognized the

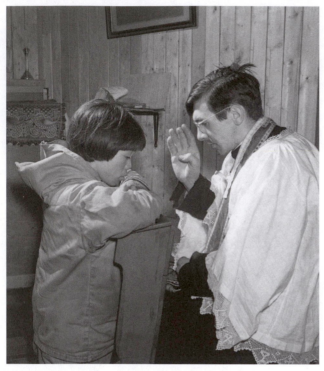

Inuit confession. NAC, PA141738.

the Catholics generally served in the North for life, without thought of promotion. Moreover, the Catholics—and this had been true of the French–English rivalry since its earliest days—were less squeamish about differences of race and culture. A Belgian priest, for example, did not as a rule consider Native culture inferior simply because it was not Belgian. English missionaries found it more difficult to appreciate other cultures. Bishop W.C. Bompas, who devoted his life to the First Nations of the Yukon, described the Loucheux (Gwitch'in) of the northern Yukon as 'the lowest of all people', and was repelled by what he perceived as their unclean and shiftless ways; in describing the Dene, he mentioned their 'heathen habits of impurity'.[2] Although he clearly was devoted to his flock, it is not so clear that he regarded them as his equals; no doubt they were equal in the sight of God, but as social beings they were several steps down the ladder from a bishop of the Church of England.

Nevertheless, both sides had their successes, and these are reflected in the denominational differences that still persist in the North. The Anglicans won the allegiance of the First Nations of the Yukon and, later, the Inuit of the central and eastern Arctic, while the Roman Catholics prevailed in the Mackenzie Valley. Because Catholic missionaries tended to spend their entire careers in a single community, they generally became fluent in the local language, learned the customs, and eventually acquired a status similar to that of community elders. A few Anglicans followed the same pattern, notably Bishop Bompas, who went to the North in 1865 and lived there until his death in 1906. Others, though, did not stay long enough to learn more than a few phrases of the

inevitability of the missionary enterprise, it came down strongly on the side of the Anglicans, even threatening on occasion to cut off trade with those who converted to Catholicism. There was considerable unpleasantness in the rivalry that resulted; the Catholics accused the Anglicans of heresy and of spreading slanderous stories about their sexual lives, the Anglicans accused the Catholics of other calumnies, and the general nastiness was far from edifying.

The Catholic Church also had advantages, however. Its missionary priests were unencumbered by many of the worldly concerns of their rivals. Some Anglican missionaries served in the North with an ear perennially cocked for a 'call' from a parish in a more congenial climate;

Anglican mission, Hay River, NWT, 1922. NWT Archives, Jackson Collection, N79-004:0182.

local language. Recognizing the problem, Bompas suggested that the Anglicans should rely on missionaries from the lower social classes in Britain, whose status would be so elevated by becoming missionaries that they would not want to leave: 'those of an inferior grade in going to the far [north]west generally rise a peg which is mostly pleasant to themselves and their neighbours.'[3]

Allegiance to a church is one thing, and there were plenty of baptisms and confirmations, but the real effects of the introduction of Christianity in the North are difficult to assess. After all, Christianity differed in fundamental ways from Native spiritual beliefs. The former was a highly structured code of faith and belief (or, more correctly, a number of competing codes); the latter were loose and difficult to define. Christianity did not teach a great deal about this world, but rather how one should live in order to gain a better one; Native beliefs were centred in the natural life of this world and its other-worldly ramifications. This meant that it was a tremendous leap to abandon Aboriginal beliefs in favour of Christianity; on the other hand, one did not necessarily have to do so, since the two systems were so different that it was quite possible to believe in both of them. Missionaries such as Bompas were convinced that 'paganism' had to be rooted out of Native people, since any remaining trace would taint their Christian beliefs, but most of his flock did not agree. Native people could either maintain two sepa-

The Coast Guard ship *Labrador* approaching Pond Inlet, NWT, September 1968. NWT Archives, Smith Collection, N91-028:0291.

rate belief systems, as many did, or combine elements of both; this kind of syncretism is gaining favour among many Native people today. Believing in both systems, or combining them, worked well for the First Nations. Some Dene shamans, for instance, became lay readers for the church, thereby retaining their role as community spiritual leaders. And when starvation, disease, or other calamities visited them, the people could choose to ask either the missionaries or the shamans for help, according to circumstances.

Some historians have argued that the First Nations were forced into Christianity by the collapse of their own societies. According to John Webster Grant, in *Moon of Wintertime*,

'Conversion to Christianity was essentially a phenomenon of the moon of wintertime, when ancestral spirits had ceased to perform their expected functions.' This idea may have some validity for indigenous people elsewhere, but it is not true of the Native people of northern Canada. A better analysis is provided by the historian Kerry Abel, who concludes of the Dene that they

> were not easily, automatically, and happily 'converted' to Christianity or to other values which the Christian missionaries attempted to teach. Some rejected the message entirely and openly, some listened cautiously and politely so as not to offend, still others adopted elements of

Indian residential school at Carcross, *c*. 1920. Anglican Church Archives, P7538-892.

Christian teaching which seemed appropriate to individual cases. There was no single response in this individualistic society. As a pragmatic people, they tested the new ideas and accepted only those which proved their utility.[4]

In the long run, however, the missionary activity that caused the most controversy in northern Canada was not theological but educational. It was the missionaries who set up the first schools north of the 60th parallel, and until a generation ago, it was the missionaries who ran them. The arrangement by which they did so was advantageous both for the religious denominations and for the government. From the government's point of view, it permitted the discharge of their obligation to educate Native people at the lowest possible cost, since the missionary teachers, especially the Roman Catholics, worked for almost nothing. From the point of view of the churches, the government support for the schools was a subsidy that permitted intense proselytizing of young Native people during their most impressionable years.

The missionaries were quite frank about the purpose of education: it was to eradicate what they considered the unwholesome aspects of Native culture—in the case of the Inuit, for example, the practices of wife-sharing and infanticide—and to replace them with what Bishop Bompas called 'the blessings of civilization'. Even a century ago, however, there were

Divine service at Cape Wolstenholme, 1933. HBC Archives, N7837.

some who wondered what these blessings were, and there was a strong body of opinion that the First Nations people were better left alone, that education would ruin them for their traditional life without preparing them for any useful alternative. When the Anglican Church petitioned the federal government in 1908 to provide more money for Native education in the Yukon—one in a long string of such requests—the minister of the Interior, Frank Oliver, replied: 'I will not undertake in a general way to educate the Indians of the Yukon. In my judgement they can, if left as Indians, earn a better living.' Nevertheless, the political influence of the churches was strong enough to keep the schools open.

After 1900 both churches opened boarding schools in the main northern communities: the Anglicans at Carcross in the Yukon and the Catholics at Hay River and Aklavik, NWT. They also operated day schools and seasonal schools to teach children the rudiments of reading and writing when their families gathered in large groups for the summer. These last schools also taught adults; the average age of the pupils in one held at Teslin in 1909 was twenty. But until the end of the Second World War and the advent of the welfare state (see Chapter 9), fewer than half the Native children of school age were actually attending school at any one time. In the first half of the 1930s, only 44 per cent of eligible children were attending day school, and in the NWT the figure was much lower.

Apart from any spiritual benefits such education may have offered, which are difficult to assess, its secular effects were both good and bad. It did teach many First Nations children how to read, write, and perform basic arithmetical calculations, skills that helped them in their dealings with traders and government officials; perhaps it opened a wider world for them. Certainly the reminiscences of those who attended the boarding schools in the 1920s and 1930s are not all negative. Some of the graduates got mainstream jobs: two boys who trained on the Carcross boarding school's printing press were hired by a printing firm in Whitehorse. Johnny Johns, also a graduate of Carcross, became a businessman in the region and eventually the best (and the only Native) big-game guide in the Yukon. But these were the exceptions. The schools' insistence on the inferiority of Native culture left their students in a limbo between two worlds. Frank Oliver put the matter clearly in 1908:

> To teach an Indian child that his parents are degraded beyond measure and that whatever they did or thought was wrong could only result in the child becoming . . . admittedly and unquestionably very much less desirable a member of society than their parents who never saw the schools.[5]

The main problem was that educating Native children in the mainstream culture deprived them of the ability to survive in their own culture; yet because of racist hiring practices, there were few opportunities for them in white society. A summer missionary at Carmacks, Yukon, noted in 1934 that such children were 'potential outcasts of their own people and are not quite up to the standards of the white intellect. In other words, they are "betwixt and between"—a condition of pitiful helplessness.'[6] When Alice French, an Inuit woman born in the Mackenzie Delta in 1930 and given the name Masak, returned to her people after six years at boarding school, she had learned skills that were useless to her on the land but forgotten—or never learned—the skills she needed to survive and fulfil her responsibilities as a wife and mother. Her memoirs, *My Name Is Masak*,[7] depict her painful and difficult re-education. Whether the spiritual and other benefits of Christian education were enough to outweigh the pain that accompanied it is one of the most important topics of debate in the contemporary North.

For the fur traders, the North was a frontier to be explored and exploited. For some missionaries also it was a frontier, one where they fought the forces of darkness for the souls of the heathen. For other missionaries, however, the North did become a homeland, and this has been particularly true in the modern era. A good example is Father René Fumoleau, a priest who served the Dene of the Mackenzie Valley for many decades, and who not only spent his entire adult life bringing them spiritual guidance, but also served as a practical champion in their hour of greatest need, during the Mackenzie Valley pipeline controversy of the mid-1970s.[8]

CHAPTER FIVE

The Age of Exploration

*T*he era of exploration in northern Canada, which began a thousand years ago with Leif Ericsson and still continues today, though in a much different form, falls into roughly three periods. The first, which lasted until the early years of the nineteenth century, was motivated mostly by economic goals—first the search for the Northwest Passage, which it was hoped would bring the riches of the Orient to the fortunate European country that found it, and later the search for new fur-trade opportunities. The second period, which lasted for about a hundred years, from 1820 until after the First World War, had national pride as its basic motivation. Expeditions still tried to find the Northwest Passage, or, after its discovery in 1850, to traverse it, but the reasons were no longer economic. Now the purpose, as in the case of the competition to reach the North Pole, was simply to be the first to do it. Such endeavours were rather like the effort to put men on the moon in the 1960s: everyone knew where the moon was, and had a good idea what it was made of, so there was no real scientific or economic gain to be achieved in going there; nevertheless, the drive to be first was intense.

Today, in the third period, the word 'exploration' is really a misnomer, for in almost all cases the men, and often women, who strive to be the first to reach the pole on skis, or by snowmobile, or by dragging their own sleds, do so to challenge themselves, or in the hope of attracting media attention. Those who participate in such stunts often try to give them a scientific gloss by taking meteorological observations, or to dignify them by using them to raise money for worthy causes. It is still not easy to walk to the North Pole, but it is no longer unusual.

The most important period of exploration in Canada's North overlapped the first two periods. Beginning in the late eighteenth century, with the last of the trade-motivated expeditions, it continued throughout the nineteenth century, ending when the Canadian Arctic Expedition of 1913–18 explored the last unknown islands of the high Arctic archipelago. Beginning in 1770 with the travels of Samuel Hearne and ending 150 years later with those of Vilhjalmur Stefansson, this era saw the entire Canadian North explored and added to the world's maps, from the Barrens of the Northwest Territories to the extreme north of Ellesmere Island.

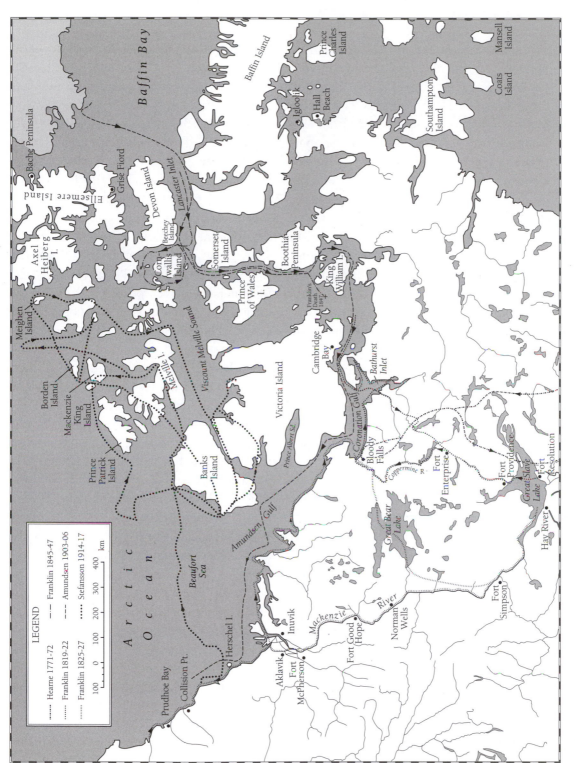

LEGEND

- ----- Hearne 1771-72
- ········ Franklin 1819-22
- ········ Franklin 1825-27
- --- Franklin 1845-47
- --- Amundsen 1903-06
- ······· Stefansson 1914-17

100 0 100 200 300 400 km

Arctic Ocean

Baffin Bay

Beaufort Sea

Bache Peninsula

Ellesmere Island

Axel Heiberg I.

Grise Fiord

Devon Island

Lancaster Inlet

Beechey Island

Cornwallis Island

Somerset Island

Boothia Peninsula

Prince of Wales I.

Meighen Island

Borden Island

Mackenzie King Island

Melville I.

Viscount Melville Sound

Prince Patrick Island

Banks Island

Prince Albert Sd.

Victoria Island

Franklin's death 1847

King William I.

Cambridge Bay

Bathurst Inlet

Coronation Gulf

Bloody Falls

Coppermine R.

Fort Enterprise

Great Bear Lake

Amundsen Gulf

Prudhoe Bay

Collision Pt.

Herschel I.

Aklavik

Fort McPherson

Inuvik

Fort Good Hope

Mackenzie River

Norman Wells

Fort Simpson

Fort Providence

Great Slave Lake

Fort Resolution

Hay River

Baffin Island

Prince Charles Island

Southampton Island

Coats Island

Mansell Island

Igloolik

Hall Beach

Exploration

Samuel Hearne (1745–92) was born in London, the son of an engineer, and joined the Royal Navy at the age of eleven. He served throughout the Seven Years' War, and after leaving the navy joined the Hudson's Bay Company, carrying trade goods and supplies between England and Fort Prince of Wales at what is now Churchill, Manitoba. When Hearne joined the company, it was under strong criticism for not being aggressive enough in its trading. Its original mandate was to trade throughout the watershed of the bay after which it was named, but although it had made some attempts earlier in the 1700s to find the Northwest Passage and conduct other explorations, for the most part it had been content to 'sleep by the frozen ocean', as its critics put it, merely operating forts on the shores of the bay. In the 1760s, however, as we have seen, aggressive fur traders from Montreal began to penetrate the northwest by land and to cut off the HBC's trade from behind.

By 1770, therefore, it had become necessary for the Hudson's Bay Company to move from the bay into the interior to establish new trading posts and take advantage of whatever other economic opportunities might present themselves. At that time, rumours had reached the company of rich deposits of native copper—nuggets of pure copper that needed no refining—lying on the ground far to the northwest of Fort Prince of Wales. In 1762 Moses Norton, the chief factor at the fort, had sent two Indians to find out the truth of the rumour. In 1767 they returned with a lump of copper and a rough map of the route to the Coppermine River. Two years later, Hearne was selected to go and confirm the information, and to locate the exact site of the copper deposit.

Hearne made three attempts to carry out his task. Setting out first in November 1769, he returned shortly thereafter when his Native guides, selected by Norton, abandoned him. He tried again in February 1770, but the party lost its way near Dubawnt Lake in the Barrens, and Hearne was robbed by passing Indians. At the end of that year he made his third attempt. This time he was lucky, or astute, enough to select as his guide Matonabbee (1737–82), a Chipewyan, born at Fort Prince of Wales, who was familiar with the worlds of both the English traders and the region's First Nations. Having served the company by making peace between the Chipewyan and the Cree of the Lake Athabasca region, whose quarrels had disrupted the fur trade, Matonabbee had also travelled as far as the Coppermine River, and was likely one of the Indians sent there by Moses Norton in 1762, though the records do not mention his name in connection with that expedition.

The Hearne/Matonabbee expedition, which took thirty-two months, from December 1770 until their return to Fort Prince of Wales at the end of June 1772, is one of the epic achievements of exploration in the Canadian North. Its remarkable success lay not in the discovery of new riches, for they found only a single piece of copper, weighing about two kilograms; apparently the Native people had been using it for centuries to make knives and other implements, and it was almost all gone. Rather, the achievement lay in the feat of traversing such a tremendous distance—more than 6,000 kilometres—through difficult country, mostly on foot, and returning alive. Much of the credit for this success belonged to Matonabbee. He insisted that the expedition not follow a European model, according to which the party would have proceeded directly to their goal in as straight a line as possible. Rather, he forced Hearne to conform to a Native model: instead of heading straight for the Coppermine, the expedition followed the caribou in their seasonal migration. When they finally arrived, in July 1771, it was obvious to Hearne that there was little copper there, and that the Coppermine River was unsuitable for navigation.

Not far from the coast, at a steep rapids later named Bloody Falls, an event occurred that for its stark drama is unequalled by anything in the history of the North. Hearne and his party had been instructed to deal peacefully with any Inuit they might encounter. Yet when the group arrived at Bloody Falls and found a group of Inuit encamped there, Matonabbee and his men immediately prepared for attack. At one o'clock on the morning of 17 July, their approach masked by the noise of the falls, they crept up on the sleeping Inuit. Hearne's record of what happened next is one of the most harrowing narratives in northern Canadian history:

The shrieks and groans of the poor expiring wretches were truly dreadful; and my horror was much increased at seeing a young girl, seemingly about eighteen years of age, killed so near me, that when the first spear was stuck into her side she fell down at my feet, and twisted round my legs, so that it was with difficulty that I could disengage myself from her dying grasps. As two Indian men pursued the unfortunate victim, I solicited very hard for her life; but the murderers made no reply till they had stuck both their spears through her body, and transfixed her to the ground. They then looked me sternly in the face, and began to ridicule me, by asking if I wanted an Esquimaux wife; and paid not the smallest regard to the shrieks and agony of the poor wretch, who was twining round their spears like an eel! Indeed, after receiving much abusive language from them on the occasion, I was at length obliged to desire that they would be more expeditious in dispatching their victim out of her misery, otherwise I should be obliged, out of pity, to assist in the friendly office of putting an end to the existence of a fellow-creature who was so cruelly wounded. On this request being made, one of the Indians hastily drew his spear from the place where it was first lodged, and pierced it through her breast near the heart. . . . My situation and the terror of my mind at beholding this butchery, cannot easily be conceived, much less described . . . even at this hour [nearly twenty years later] I cannot reflect on the transactions of that horrid day without shedding tears.

When the savages discovered that the surviving Esquimaux had gained the shore . . . [they] began to plunder the tents of the deceased of all the copper utensils they could find . . . after which they assembled on the top of an adjacent high hill, and standing all in a cluster, so as to form a solid circle, with their spears erect in the air, gave many shouts of victory, constantly clashing their spears against each other, and frequently calling out tima! tima! [a phrase meaning, in the language of the victims, 'what cheer?'] by way of derision to the poor surviving Esquimaux, who were standing on the shoal almost knee-deep in water.[1]

Bloody Falls on the Coppermine River, the site of the most terrible episode in Samuel Hearne's book, photographed in 1948. NWT Archives, Osborne Collection, N90-006:0138.

This expedition was the crowning event of Hearne's life. In 1774 he travelled to the interior to found the first of the HBC's inland posts, Cumberland House, in what is now northern Saskatchewan. Put in charge of Fort Prince of Wales in 1776, he suffered the indignity of having to surrender it to a French force in 1782, an event that led Matonabbee to commit suicide. Hearne retired in 1787 and spent the last years of his life preparing his journals for publication. Appearing in 1795, *A Journey from Prince of Wales's Fort, in Hudson's Bay, to the Northern Ocean . . .* gained him a reputation as an accomplished writer. Had all those who

penetrated the Arctic in the next century followed Hearne's example of accommodation to the land and its people, perhaps more of them would have lived to write their own memoirs.

The other explorer from this era is more famous, perhaps because a great river is named after him, though his travels were not nearly so arduous as Hearne's. Born in Scotland in 1764, Alexander Mackenzie was taken to America at the age of ten by his father, a farmer who had suffered economic reverses, and later, when the revolution broke out, he was sent to Montreal for schooling. In 1779, when he was fifteen, he followed the path of hundreds of his countrymen and joined a fur-trading company—not the Hudson's Bay Company but a Montreal rival, one of the firms that had sprung up to take over the old French fur business after the British conquest.

Mackenzie spent some time as assistant to Peter Pond (1740–1807), the violent and eccentric American-born trader who was the first European to cross the Methye Portage to the Athabasca, opening the Athabasca country to the overland fur trade in the 1770s and becoming the first to carry the trade into the Arctic watershed. E.E. Rich, the leading historian of the Hudson's Bay Company, estimated that Pond brought 80,000 beaver pelts out of the Athabasca country in 1779, a tremendous coup for the Canadian traders. It was Pond who first suggested that there was a great river flowing out of the Lake Athabasca–Slave River system—and that it was the one that flowed into the Pacific at Cook Inlet in Alaska. The idea of finding an easy river route to the Pacific fired the imaginations of the Montreal traders, not because they wanted the honour of finding a Northwest Passage by canoe, but because of the rich virgin fur lands that such a route would open up. For Alexander Mackenzie, it was also a tremendous chance for adventure.

On 3 June 1789 Mackenzie set out from Fort Chipewyan, a post recently established on the south shore of Lake Athabasca, with four French-Canadian voyageurs, a young German, a Chipewyan known as the 'English Chief', and a number of Native men and women. They had some trouble with ice in the Slave River and Great Slave Lake, but once they got into the great river itself, the trip was remarkably smooth. For 500 kilometres the river

Sir Alexander Mackenzie (1764–1820), the first European to traverse Canada by land and to explore the river that now bears his name. The National Gallery of Canada, Ottawa, Canadian War Memorials Collection.

trended west, and it seemed that the expedition would indeed reach the Pacific. But then its course turned due north. Realizing that he was heading for the Arctic Ocean, not the Pacific, Mackenzie pushed on nevertheless, to 'satisfy Peoples Curiosity tho' not their Intentions'. On 12 July the party reached the ocean. In fact, conditions were so foggy that at first they were not even sure they had done so, but at a place they named Whale Island they finally saw the rise and fall of the tide, and a pod of white whales. Having descended the

Sir John Franklin in a heroic pose. NAC, C1352..

short time; it took him just a month and a day to return from salt water to Fort Chipewyan.

Mackenzie spent his life in the fur trade, eventually becoming an important figure in the North West Company. He retired to Scotland around 1811, married (at the age of forty-eight) a girl of fourteen, and died eight years later. His pioneering journey to the Mackenzie River, though an easy feat compared with Hearne's, had more important results, for after the North West Company was absorbed by the Hudson's Bay Company in 1821, the revitalized company expanded into the Mackenzie Valley, establishing a string of posts— including Fort Simpson and Fort Norman— all the way north to Fort McPherson, established in 1840 on the edge of the Mackenzie River Delta.

The most famous explorer in the history of northern Canada is without doubt Sir John Franklin (1786–1847). It is ironic that this should be the case, but given the public taste in such things, perhaps it is not surprising. Franklin's fame rests not on his skill, nor on his achievements, but mostly on the fact that his last expedition was a disaster and his fate a 'mystery' in that no one knows exactly how and where he died. This is a pity, for there were other explorers far more successful than he, and the concentration on his last expedition overshadows some considerable earlier successes in his own career. Franklin was the son of an English textile merchant, and joined the British navy over his parents' objections at the age of fourteen. After participating in the Battle of Copenhagen (1801), he served on an expedition to chart the coast of Australia, where he was wrecked near Sydney and stranded for six weeks on a sandbar. Returning

1,700-km river in only fourteen days, by 12 September they were back at Fort Chipewyan.

Mackenzie's trip, like Hearne's, brought no immediate commercial gain to its backers, and it was rumoured (though apparently without foundation) that his own name for the river was 'the River Disappointment'. In 1792, however, he had a second chance to try for the Pacific, and this time he succeeded. Starting again at Fort Chipewyan, Mackenzie headed west, up the Peace River to its headwaters, across a height of land to the Fraser, and then across another portage to the Bella Coola and the Pacific. This trip too was completed in a very home after an absence of two years, he re-joined the navy, in which he served until 1815, reaching the rank of lieutenant and taking part in the battle of New Orleans.

At the end of the war, still not thirty years old, Franklin was pensioned off on half-pay, like hundreds of other naval officers. Some of these men went to Canada or one of the other colonies; Susanna Moodie's husband was one example, as was the father of Sir Sam Steele, the famous Mounted Policeman. Franklin was spared the fate of roughing it in the Canadian bush, however, when he was chosen in 1818, probably on the strength of his war record and his voyage to Australia, to participate in an important British expedition to find the Northwest Passage. This expedition marked the beginning of the century in which the process of exploration became purely a matter of national honour. Men now went to the passage as they would go a century later to Mount Everest, not for any consideration of profit, but simply because it was there.

The 1818 expedition, which tried to cross the Arctic Ocean from Spitsbergen to Asia, was a failure, proving only that a navigable route could not be forced through the Arctic pack ice. In 1819 Franklin was put in charge of an expedition that was to sail into Hudson Bay, travel overland along the Arctic coast to the Coppermine River, and map the coast to the east of the river. Nearly fifty years had passed since Hearne had reached the Arctic coast, yet he and Mackenzie were the only Europeans to have visited it, and most of the region was still a blank on the map. Hastily and badly planned (though this was not Franklin's fault), the expedition accomplished a modest amount of mapping; however, nine men died (a tenth,

Franklin, photographed sometime before 19 May 1845, the date of his departure on his last voyage. A very early photograph, perhaps the first taken of a person important to northern Canadian history. National Maritime Museum, UK, 9191(A).

suspected of cannibalism, shot an officer and was himself executed), and Franklin lost the respect of his men. Though his record as an explorer was mixed, he had character, a quality that the British valued extremely highly. Brave and tenacious, he became a hero in much the same mould as Sir Robert Scott, the hero of the Antarctic, who shared some of Franklin's characteristics and who met the same fate. In 1825, on a third expedition, this time to explore the Arctic coast east and west of the Mackenzie Delta, Franklin managed to

'House Built by the Franklin Expedition, Simpson', photographed in 1922. NWT Archives, Jackson Collection, N79-004:0193.

chart more than 500 kilometres of previously unexplored coastline, and returned home to wide acclaim. After serving another four years in the navy, in 1837 he was appointed lieutenant-governor of Tasmania, then called Van Diemen's Land, but fell afoul of political intrigue and was recalled in 1843.

The last act of Franklin's life began in 1845. By then the coast of the Canadian Arctic and the southern part of the Arctic archipelago had been quite thoroughly covered, and only a 500-km stretch remained unexplored. The location of the Northwest Passage was fairly clear, since ships had sailed into both ends of it; all that was left to do was traverse it. Franklin was 58 and somewhat corpulent when he set out on his last expedition, but he was the leading Arctic explorer of his generation, and had strong friends in the Admiralty. He sailed in May 1845, heading for Lancaster Sound and the Passage; in July his ships, the *Erebus* and the *Terror*, were sighted by whalers in Baffin Bay. He was never seen again, nor did any news of the expedition reach Britain until 1850.

Reckoning that character and firm leadership would see Englishmen through any difficulty, the British had made doubly sure of success by providing the Franklin expedition with the latest in technological assistance. The ships carried large quantities of canned provisions, the seams soldered, as it later turned out, with lead that leached into the food. The ships were heated by pipes fired from steam boilers; there was china, crystal, a library, and other recreational material. What the expedition did not carry, however, was anything that smacked of indigenous technology: there were no dogs, or sleds, or pemmican, let alone Inuit clothes—the men were outfitted with the usual British navy issue of wool serge. This last is hard to understand unless one appreciates the British way of looking at things in that era. Here it may help to remember that sixty years later Robert Scott declined to take dogs to the South Pole—where he could have used them for transport on the way there and if necessary eaten them on the way back—because that would not have been sporting. For Sir John Franklin to dress in caribou skins and eat seal meat like an Inuk would have been to let down the side; it would have been an act of race betrayal.

Notwithstanding the popular perception, there is no real mystery about the fate of the Franklin expedition. Two brief messages found later in cairns told all that mattered. The two ships had got well into the Northwest Passage, heading in the right direction, but in 1846 they became locked in pack ice northwest of King William Island. The party had no alternative but to wait out the winter and hope to escape in the spring. But Franklin died in 1847—the cause of death was not recorded—and the ice did not thaw. More men died, and in 1848 the survivors abandoned the ships, trekking southeast in the vain hope of reaching a settlement—but the nearest one was hundreds of kilometres away. The doomed party consisted of Captain Crozier and 104 men who had survived two years in the ice. On 25 April 1848 Crozier left a message in a cairn on the northwest coast of King William Island with the news that

Captain Francis Crozier, who took command after Franklin's death and led his crew in an unsuccessful attempt to reach help. National Maritime Museum, UK, 9191(I).

Franklin and 23 others had died. For a time the men dragged boats across the ice containing silverware, delftware tea cups, and other useless artefacts; why they did this is difficult to imagine, unless their reasoning had been affected by the toxic lead in the food cans. Some time later the party, now numbering 40, met a group of four Inuit families, who many years later told what happened:

Crozier approached them, beseeching them with gestures to open their packs. They held seal meat out to him. He took the meat and

began eating and indicated the Eskimos should give meat to the other men, which they did. They spent the night with Crozier's party. In the morning Crozier pleaded with them to stay, saying over and over the word he thought meant 'seal'. But the families walked away. The thin resources of that part of the Arctic would not support the four families and a party of forty men, and the Eskimos knew it.[2]

Franklin's disappearance stimulated the greatest spurt of Arctic exploration in Canadian history. No fewer than thirty expeditions searched for him between 1847 and 1859, some backed by the British navy, some by Americans (one rich American merchant named Henry Grinnell paid for two of them; he got his name on the map of the High Arctic), and some by Lady Franklin, who raised money for searches and played a notable public role as the tragic widow of the fallen hero—a role successfully reprised by Lady Scott sixty years later. The interest in Franklin among northern enthusiasts remains unabated. In the past dozen years, an expedition has found the graves of two of his crew members, exhumed the frozen bodies, and found traces of toxic substances in their hair. The late folksinger Stan Rogers wrote an evocative song about Franklin and the Northwest Passage. Several books have been written about the expedition, the most innovative one, by David Woodman, a study of how stories about it have been preserved in the oral tradition of the Inuit of the region. Because his body has never been found, Franklin remains in the select company—some respectable (Amelia Earhart), others unsavoury (Jimmy Hoffa)—of those whose fate will likely remain a 'mystery'. Franklin's weaknesses are fairly summed

up by Clive Holland in the *Dictionary of Canadian Biography*:

Franklin's characteristics as a pious, diffident, gentle, and in some ways awkward man who nevertheless found great reserves of moral and physical strength in the face of terrible suffering combined to lend him an aura of greatness. . . . But . . . those same characteristics have indicated his weaknesses as an explorer. His style was to lead by personal charm and by moral example, but in difficult times this was no substitute for a more authoritative kind of leadership. . . . His courage was admirable, but a more accomplished explorer . . . would have avoided the circumstances that called for such courage. . . . he was slow to learn and slower still to adapt to unexpected circumstances. His determination to succeed was unwavering but was blended with an extreme loyalty to duty—with a dangerous tendency blindly to carry out instructions. This tendency was a major failing on his first expedition and may have contributed to the tragedy of his last.

After the failures and contradictions of Franklin's life, it is pleasant to turn to the lives of men who were unqualified successes as explorers. The five best-known in the late nineteenth and early twentieth centuries were Peary, Nansen, Amundsen, Sverdrup, and Stefansson. Of these, the American Robert Peary (1856–1920) deserves the least consideration as an explorer. Though fascinating, perhaps, as a ruthless monomaniac, he was less an explorer than a man obsessed with a single goal—being the first to reach the North Pole—and careless about whom he exploited to achieve it. The other four were all of Nordic descent: Fridtjof Nansen (1861–1930), whose achievements took place in the Arctic Ocean rather than in Canada proper, was a Norwegian, as were Roald Amundsen (1872–1928), and Otto Sverdrup (1854–1930), and Vilhjalmur Stefansson (1879–1962) was born in Canada of Icelandic parents. All these men readily adopted the technology developed by the Inuit over the centuries: dressing in skin clothing, travelling where the food was rather than along a preconceived path, and using dogs and sleds. All of them demonstrated that, given such technology, along with a reasonable amount of luck, Europeans could survive the worst Arctic conditions in some degree of comfort.

In a voyage lasting three seasons, 1903–5, Roald Amundsen and the crew of the *Gjoa* finally achieved the centuries-old goal of traversing the Northwest Passage. He succeeded where so many others had failed mostly because of the professional nature of his preparations. He trained himself to be a competent ship's captain so that he would not have to share command, took with him a small crew, all experts in some useful skill, and followed in detail the Inuit methods of living off the land. It was supremely ironic that his ship was frozen in the ice in the same general region as Franklin's: he and his crew lived well for two winters off what the land provided, studying the Inuit and making scientific observations on the same island where Franklin's crew had starved to death fifty years earlier. They were, however, frozen in the pack ice for two consecutive winters, demonstrating conclusively what had been surmised for a long time—that the Northwest Passage was not reliable enough to be a practical shipping route. Amundsen later applied his principles of exploration with

Roald Amundsen (1872–1928), the first to bring a ship through the Northwest Passage and the first to reach the South Pole; arguably the most able Arctic explorer who ever lived. NAC c04073.

Vilhjalmur Stefansson (1879–1962), the successful though controversial Canadian-born Arctic explorer and discoverer. NAC c086406

Inspector Henry Larsen (1899–1964), born in Norway, joined the RCMP in 1928 and commanded the police patrol ship *St. Roch* in Arctic waters for twenty years. His ship was the first (1940–42) to navigate the Northwest Passage from west to east, the first to make the passage in both directions, and the first to circumnavigate North America. It is now preserved at the Vancouver Maritime Museum. NAC, c70771.

spectacular success to a race for the South Pole, easily beating the hapless Robert Scott.

Otto Sverdrup, a Norwegian sailor and outdoorsman, had served with Nansen on an 1888 expedition to the interior of Greenland, and had captained Nansen's ship, the *Fram*, when, as an experiment, it was put into the polar pack ice to drift across the Arctic Ocean in 1893–96. Between 1898 and 1902 he made a remarkable expedition to Ellesmere Island, in the course of which he crossed and mapped all the major islands in the high Arctic archipelago. Three of them, Axel Heiberg, Ellef Ringnes, and Amund Ringnes, he discovered and named after his financial backers (the Ringnes brothers were brewers). He also claimed these islands for Norway, and since his claim as their discoverer was unquestioned, this cast Canada's sovereignty over them into question. Sverdrup, like Amundsen, adopted Inuit techniques, travelling thousands of kilometres without starvation or loss of life, and his achievement was all the more notable because, unlike Amundsen, he left the security of his ship and travelled extensively on the land and sea ice.

The most controversial among this Nordic quartet, and the best-known in his day, was Vilhjalmur Stefansson. Born in what is now Manitoba and raised in the United States, he was educated as an ethnologist, and visited the Arctic for the first time as a member of an expedition to the Beaufort Sea in 1906. He immediately fell in love with the Arctic and determined to make it the focus of his life. What made him famous, and controversial, was his genius for publicity and self-promotion. He announced what came to be known as the Stefansson method of Arctic exploration, which was essentially to live off the land and to use Aboriginal methods to do so; in this way, Stefansson often said, the Arctic would become not the end of the earth, but a 'polar Mediterranean', where one could live in comfort and safety. This was not an original idea—Nansen, Sverdrup, and Amundsen had proven its wisdom long before Stefansson crossed the Arctic Circle—but Stefansson preached it for

An RCMP officer exercising his dog team on the Yukon River, 1927. Yukon Archives, Allard Collection, 82H02 H-58 #53.

years on the North American lecture circuit, where the others, as foreigners, were at a disadvantage. He also knew how to give press reporters a good story. After his second expedition, in 1908, he announced that the Inuit of Victoria Island had lighter complexions and hair than other Inuit, and speculated that they might be descended from the original Norse settlers of Greenland. The Victoria Inuit were soon dubbed the 'blond Eskimos', a term that brought Stefansson fame and some embarrassment, since it turned out not to be true: there were Inuit who were somewhat lighter-complexioned than others, but they were by no means blond. The story also aroused envy and ill-feeling from other anthropologists who were not courted by the press.

Stefansson achieved fame at a time when the Canadian government was feeling increasingly uncomfortable about its passive attitude towards northern sovereignty. When he approached Ottawa in search of financing for a large Arctic expedition, the government loosened the purse strings and authorized the Canadian Arctic Expedition of 1913–18, an enterprise whose main purpose was to explore the remaining islands of the western Arctic and to make a through study of the Inuit. It was the

RCMP officer boiling water for tea on patrol somewhere in the Yukon, 1932. Yukon Archives, Allard Collection, 82/402 H-58 #124.

first and last major multi-year expedition officially sponsored by the Canadian government, and although it achieved a number of successes, it was dogged by controversy. Right at the outset a disaster occurred when the expedition's ship *Karluk*, which some had warned was inadequate, became trapped in the ice north of Alaska. Stefansson left it to go hunting on the shore, and was prevented by ice conditions from returning. In the meantime the ship was carried westward with the twenty-five crew members who had remained on board. Floating north of Russia, it was again caught in the ice and crushed. One group of

five set off on their own and were never heard from again; another four died on Herald Island. The remaining sixteen, five of them Inuit, reached Wrangel Island, a Russian island north of Siberia, where three died, one by suicide, before they were rescued.

Ordered by the government to abandon the expedition, Stefansson refused. Over the next four years he explored the western Arctic, discovering a number of good-sized islands (Borden, Meighen, Mackenzie King) and effectively completing the map of the Canadian archipelago. But on his return he found that he was *persona non grata* with the government, which was further embarrassed when he made an entirely unfounded claim, on behalf of Canada, to Wrangel Island. Furthermore, in 1921 he engineered a four-man expedition to this unimportant island, which he saw as a central point in his polar Mediterranean, in the course of which all four (Stefansson did not go himself) died.

Stefansson spent the rest of his long life writing popular books on the Arctic, lecturing, and promoting various visionary schemes for northern development, including an ill-fated attempt to start a domestic reindeer industry. He quite correctly predicted that the polar basin would become an important route for transcontinental air travel; he scarcely could have foreseen, however, that improvements in the range of aircraft and innovations such as radar would make it unnecessary to build facilities on the ground to accommodate such developments. He also predicted, so far incorrectly, that the polar basin would become an important trade route. In the last years of his life he taught at Dartmouth College, New Hampshire, where he became a resident sage, inspiring students with accounts of his northern experiences and in snowy weather showing them how to build igloos on the college lawn. He was a man who aroused strong feelings: his many friends called him 'Stef', while his many enemies called him 'Windjammer'. Even after his death in 1962, some veterans of his expeditions could hardly pronounce his name without a curse. Whatever his faults, however, it is worth noting that of all the long list of explorers mentioned in this chapter, he was the only one to whom it occurred that the North might be a homeland rather than simply a frontier to be explored, endured, or conquered. In this Stefansson was much closer to the North's indigenous people than any of his contemporaries.

CHAPTER SIX

Eldorado

*I*n the last years of the nineteenth century, an event occurred that once again riveted the attention of the world on the Canadian North. The discovery of gold near what is now Dawson City in the summer of 1896 led to the Klondike gold rush of 1897–99, and eventually made the most westerly region of the North a part of the modern world.

The Klondike gold rush is one of the most melodramatic episodes in Canadian history— a history that is notably lacking in the kind of freewheeling, dramatic action associated with the history of the American West. In fact many people, then and now, confused by the geography of the far northwest and the theatrical nature of the story, think that the Klondike cannot be Canadian; the Dawson City post office still receives mail addressed to 'Dawson, Alaska'. It was the quintessential frontier episode in the history of the Canadian North. No Klondiker ever 'emigrated' to the Yukon, or even 'moved' there—both terms imply a permanence that no gold-seeker ever intended; they simply went there, fully intending to leave once their fortune was made.

The world was surprised when gold was discovered in the Yukon, but it should not have been: the great discovery was really no more than the last of the great finds in the mountains of western North America, of which the California gold rush of 1849 had been the first. After that first discovery, miners had been scouring the Rocky Mountains for decades on the reasonable assumption that the California lode could not be the only one. They were right, and after 1849 further great discoveries were made, notably in south-central British Columbia in 1858, in 1860 in the Cariboo country, in 1861 on the Stikine River, and ten years later in the Cassiar district of northern British Columbia. It was gold, in fact, that led to the initial settlement of the BC interior. The bright trail of gold had been drawing miners northward for twenty years before the strike on Bonanza Creek.

Among those miners were three men who arrived in the Yukon in 1872. Leroy Napoleon McQuesten, a young man from a New England farm who much preferred to be called by his nickname, 'Jack', was a likeable fellow who later came to be known as the 'Father of the Yukon'. Arthur Harper had emigrated from

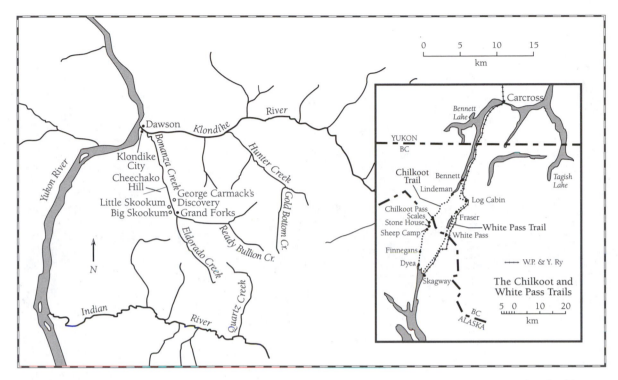

The Klondike

northern Ireland in 1832 and had been looking for gold in various places in North America since the 1850s. Arthur Mayo was a former circus acrobat from Kentucky. The three men worked part-time looking for gold, and part-time as traders. In 1874 they built a post, Fort Reliance, near an Indian village six miles downstream from the present site of Dawson City. The trade prospered, and although they did not come across any large gold deposits, they did find enough to keep them looking. Other miners trickled into the Yukon Valley, and by 1882 approximately fifty men were searching for gold and finding small but promising amounts. By the early 1890s they had grown to nearly a thousand, centred around the community of Fortymile, located where the river of the same name empties into

the Yukon. These were the men who worked out the technique of extracting gold from the frozen gravel (by burning and thawing) upon which the later gold industry would initially be based.

Fortymile, which reached its zenith in 1894, was one of the most isolated communities in North America. It depended for supplies on merchants in San Francisco, 8,000 kilometres away, who shipped their goods north on two small trading steamers belonging to the Alaska Commercial Company. Because there were no government officials in the region, the residents of Fortymile lived in a society of their own making, a 'community of hermits whose one common bond was their mutual isolation', as Pierre Berton put it.[1] It was mostly a male society, though some men

The twenty men of the first Mounted Police detachment north of the 60th parallel, photographed at Fortymile in 1895 or 1896. Inspector Charles Constantine, in the round hat and wing collar, commanded the detachment. Yukon Archives, G-45, 85/62.

brought their wives and children north with them, in which miners came and went as they pleased, subject only to the regulations of the 'miners' meeting', the governing body of the community.

The miners' meeting, which regulated social as well as mining issues, was an assembly of all the miners who lived in the region, and could be convened by anyone who had a grievance. The meeting would listen to all sides in a dispute, and then deliver a verdict by majority vote. The punishment was often ban-

ishment from the community. So long as the community remained a small group of people all engaged in the same pursuit, the miners' meeting functioned quite well. An example of how it worked was the case of Frank Leslie, a confidence man who in 1886 had persuaded four experienced miners in Seattle that he knew where a rich strike of gold could be made on the Stewart River. The miners put up money and supplies, and the party travelled into the Yukon. But the story proved false, and as the men spent the winter on the Stewart

'Packers Ascending Summit of Chilkoot Pass, 1898'. Photo by E.A. Hegg, an American who took many of the best pictures of the gold rush. Author's collection.

River, the four miners discussed lynching Leslie. Fearing for his life, Leslie waited until it was his turn to cook, then dosed the food with arsenic kept on hand to poison wolves. But he used too little, and only made his victims sick. He then tried to shoot them, but was overpowered and brought before a miners' meeting. He claimed that he had acted in good faith in telling his story, and had acted in self-defence. The meeting decided that he was

an undesirable citizen, and after much discus-

sion it was decided to banish him, so he was furnished with a sled, provisions enough to get out if he could, was ordered to move up-river at least one hundred and fifty miles from that camp, and assured that if ever he was seen within that distance of it, any one then present would be justified in shooting him on sight. He left to make his way unaided up the Yukon. . . . It was thought he richly deserved punishment, but as they had no prison in which to confine him, nor any way to detain him for any length of time, all they could do was hang him or

A rare close-up of men climbing the Chilkoot Pass, this photo gives an idea of the effort involved. The trip had to be made as many as twenty times. NAC, C33462.

banish him. His death they did not want to be directly responsible for, though many of them felt they were condemning him to death in agreeing to the sentence imposed.[2]

Leslie was successful in reaching tidewater, however, and he survived. The miners' meeting as an institution did not; when a party of twenty Mounted Policemen arrived in the Yukon in the summer of 1895, one of their first acts was to ban it.

What made the Klondike rush so notable was its timing, not so much for Canada as for the rest of the world, and particularly for the United States. The 1890s was the decade of the 'closing' of the American frontier, when the US census revealed that although there was still much free land available for settlement in what are now the 'lower 48' states, for the first time since the founding of Virginia and Massachusetts, some 250 years earlier, there was no longer a continuous line of steadily advancing settlement. There was a sense that America had reached its limits, and the Klondike drew many men and women who were looking less for gold than for a new frontier with new possibilities.

The other factor that made the Klondike rush so timely was the great economic depression that gripped the industrialized world, and especially the United States, during the 1890s. Second in severity only to the depression of the 1930s, it led to, among other things, a tremendous political battle over whether the American currency should be backed by gold or could be inflated. This complex and difficult question was the main issue of the American election of 1896, with the result that gold was on everybody's mind. When huge quantities were discovered in the far northwest, the effect in the south was electric.

Had the Klondike gold been found locked in quartz and other rocks, as it is in northern Ontario and around Yellowknife, the rush would have been very different, for individual miners are not capable of extracting gold of that kind. What is needed is heavy machinery for moving and crushing large quantities of rock, each tonne of which contains only small quantities of gold. Apart from the original prospectors, individuals cannot make money from such gold unless they have large amounts of capital to invest in machinery. But the Klondike gold did not have to be extracted

Equipment was left at the summit of the pass while men went back for more. Photo taken 13 May 1898. RCMP photo 1244.

with hardrock mining techniques; it was plac-er gold, and with luck even children could eas-ily fill their pockets with it.

Placer, or alluvial, gold was once locked in rock. But over the millennia it was eroded out of the base rock as grains and small pebbles, along with grains and pebbles of ordinary rock. These were washed into creeks and rivers, but the fragments of gold, being much heavier than rock and silt, sank quickly to the bottom of creeks and were covered with muck and debris. Over the years these creeks shifted their courses; some of the gold ended up cov-ered by many feet of overburden, while some remained right at the surface, or was uncov-ered by later creeks. The Klondike district

appears on the map as a number of creeks run-ning in all directions down from a prominent hill. Many of the creeks were gold-bearing, and it is thought that the original source of the gold was in this hill, from which it had washed out in all directions. There is, therefore, no longer a mother lode in the Klondike; all the gold was long ago deposited in the creeks.

The technique was simple, though it could be arduous. The prospectors looked for gold by 'panning' the gravel in the beds of streams. This technique—which tourists visit-ing the Dawson City suburb of Guggieville can practise today—involves taking a quantity of gravel in a pie-shaped pan about two feet in diameter, filling it half-full of water, holding it

2047   YUKON DETACHMENT N.W.M.P. AT THE SUMMIT OF WHITE PASS. AUG. 8. 1899.   H.C. BARL

Mounted Police at the international boundary on the summit of the Chilkoot Pass, 8 August 1899. Yukon Archives, Beatty Collection, 82/390 H-179.

away from your body at a slight downward angle, and swirling the mixture around in such a way that the gravel will spill out of the pan in small quantities; because the gold is heavier than the gravel, it will remain when the lighter material is washed out. This technique is easily learned and works even with 'colours', or very small flakes of gold, as tourists find to their delight: every one seems to find a few small flakes, though the proprietors of this attraction swear that the gravel is not salted.

If panning showed that the area looked promising, prospectors would stake a claim and then dig down. This was where the hard work began. Because the Klondike is in the region of permafrost, the creek beds are frozen a few centimetres below the surface, even in midsummer. Hence prospectors had to thaw

Two female musk-oxen and a two-year-old calf. The animals, related to wild sheep and goats, are native to Canada and Greenland. Fred Bruemmer photo. ZX 4852.

Walrus surfacing near the shore. These animals were nearly exterminated by European whalers by 1900, and their numbers have only partially recovered. Fred Bruemmer photo. LX 3696.

Polar bears on Hudson Bay ice at sunrise. Males can weigh as much as 650 kg. Fred Bruemmer photo. sx 9893.

Drying arctic char on racks at Bathurst Inlet. Fred Bruemmer photo. BX 6146.

Summer scene along the high Arctic coast. Fred Bruemmer photo. HX 1711.

Grandmother feeding a child porridge for breakfast. Fred Bruemmer photo. BX 5938.

Interior of the Canadian Customs tent on Chilkoot Pass, *c.* 1899. Frank Charman, a customs official, is on the right.
Yukon Archives, Sanguinette Collection, 78-79 H-133.

the ground by building fires before they could scrape up the loose gravel. This process was repeated until either gold was struck or a shaft was thawed down to bedrock. If gold was found, the prospectors would start digging horizontally at that level, following the vein and thawing as they went; this was generally done in the winter, since the shafts and tunnels were likely to collapse if warm summer air

weakened them. The gravel was piled on the surface to wait for the creeks to thaw in the spring.

When warm weather came, the pile of gravel thawed in the sun and was then run through a sluice-box. This was a wooden trough roughly two metres long, placed at a slight angle. Small strips of wood, called 'riffles', were placed across the bottom of the sluice-box, then gravel

Tent city on Lake Lindeman, headwaters of the Yukon River, spring 1898. Several boats are under construction, and more are ready to be launched. Author's collection.

was shovelled into the upper end of the box and water was diverted into it. As the water washed the gravel down the length of the box, the gold fell to the bottom, where it was caught by the riffles. Periodically the water was stopped and the gold was scraped off the upper edge of the riffles. The whole process, from thawing to sluicing, was simple and cheap, and could be managed by one or two men. However, it was profitable only where the gold was plentiful, as inevitably a considerable amount escaped the sluice box. Quite soon this method was replaced by more capital-intensive methods.

The great discovery of August 1896 was made by three men: two Tagish brothers from the southern Yukon and one veteran miner. George Carmack, born in California, had been prospecting in the Yukon and Alaska for more than ten years. His partners were Skookum Jim and Dawson Charlie (also known as Tagish Charlie). Carmack did not share the prejudice against Indians that was common among miners. In fact, he was married to his partners' sister Kate, and his friendship with the Indians had earned him the nickname 'Siwash George'. This was a pejorative term; 'siwash' was the regional equivalent of 'kaffir' or 'darkie'. Later, though, when he became rich, Carmack also sought to

A fleet of boats on Lake Laberge (the modern spelling), photographed by E.A. Hegg in the spring of 1898. RCMP photo 288.

be respectable, and then he deserted Kate.

In mid-August 1896 the three men were panning on Rabbit Creek, which flows into the Klondike River a few kilometres east of Dawson City. On the 16th of the month one of them found a good-sized nugget lying near a rock. Turning over the rocks, they found gold lying in the cracks, 'thick between the flaky slabs, like cheese sandwiches', as Carmack later recalled.[3] The men shouted for joy, panned some more gold, and staked their claims, each of which, under the rules adopted by the miners' meeting, ran 500 feet (152 m) along the creek, and from 'rim-rock to rim-

rock' of the narrow valley where the creek lay. The two brothers each staked a single claim, and Carmack, as discoverer, took one more. Later, when he had deserted his wife and fallen out with her brothers, they claimed that it was Skookum Jim who had made the discovery, and that they had agreed to let Carmack take credit for it because he was white and would thus stand a better chance of having his claim recognized. It was Carmack who renamed the creek 'Bonanza', a name that was soon to become world-famous.

The three men then travelled down the Yukon River to Fortymile to register their

Superintendent S.B. Steele commanded the Mounted Police in the Yukon at the height of the gold rush. RCMP photo 1019-3.

salmon, in anticipation of the trade that would follow a great rush. He paid some earlier prospectors $10 an acre for their rights to the land, bought some cabins from the Indians, and named his town Dawson City, after George M. Dawson, the director of the Geological Survey of Canada, who had explored the region nine years earlier. He was soon selling building lots for $1,000 each.

An irony of the Klondike gold rush was that, with a few spectacular exceptions, most of the good claims were staked by men who were already in the North. Although rumours travelled quickly, solid proof of the strike did not reach the south until the spring of 1897, and by the time southern gold-seekers got to the Klondike, no earlier than the fall of that year and in most cases not until the spring of 1898, there were no claims left to be staked. In August 1896 Bonanza Creek was staked, and two weeks later another discovery was made on a small 'pup' or tributary creek named Eldorado. About fifty claims were staked on this short creek, reputedly yielding an average of half a million dollars each (about $30 million altogether), and this with the inefficient sluicing method. Gold is now worth about twenty times as much as in 1896, when it sold for US$20 per ounce, so the gold from this one creek would be worth roughly $600 million US dollars today, or $800 million Canadian.

The news of the great discovery soon spread to the other settlements of the Yukon River Valley, downstream in Alaska, and to the towns of the Alaska panhandle. Hundreds of men and women already in the north rushed to Dawson City—if not to stake a claim, then to 'mine the miners' as saloon-keepers, laundresses, hotel-keepers, barbers, or prostitutes.

claims, and within a few days the settlement was all but deserted as virtually every miner in the region descended on Bonanza Creek. By the end of month the whole creek and several of its neighbours had been staked, a rich harvest of gold was being gathered, and a small settlement was springing up a few kilometres away, at the confluence of the Klondike and Yukon Rivers. Joe Ladue, a trader as well as a prospector, staked not a creek but the tract of flat land where the Native people dried their

Mining on Hunker Creek, near Dawson City, 1900. Cribbing at the head of a mineshaft, and a windlass for hauling muck, can be seen in the centre. The curved wooden trough is a flume, carrying water to claims lower down the creek. RCMP photo 5434.

On 14 July 1897 the *Excelsior*, a steamer owned by the Alaska Commercial Company, reached San Francisco with $500,000 in gold, and on the 17th the *Portland* docked at Seattle with over $1 million's worth. Men staggered down the gangplank, grimy but smiling, bent under the weight of suitcases filled with gold. At 1897 prices the *Portland*'s cargo alone—literally a tonne of gold—represented an incredible fortune; in an era when the average industrial wage in the United States was $460

a year, an ounce of gold was worth more than two week's wages. Some of the early strikes on Bonanza and Eldorado creeks had yielded ten or more ounces per pan—half a year's wages for a factory worker, pulled out of a Yukon stream in ten minutes. This fact—or, as it was for most, this fantasy—of easy riches helps to explain the furore surrounding the Klondike gold rush.

As the news from the Pacific coast ports went out over the cables, the steamship com-

Dawson City street scene, 1898, photographed by E.A. Hegg. RCMP photo 296.

panies were swamped with inquiries, not only from the United States and Canada but from Western Europe and as far away as Australia. Within weeks, thousands were looking in atlases to find out where the Klondike was, and the merchants of Seattle, Victoria, San Francisco, and Vancouver were laying their plans to profit from the craze.

The gold-seekers—or Klondikers, as they came to be called—were not only poor folk hoping to strike it rich. A good number of well-to-do people made the trip simply because the spirit of the late Victorian period made it almost obligatory for a man with

'pluck' to pursue the opportunities available in the 'colonies'.

There were many ways to get to Dawson City. The easiest, and the most costly, was to buy a ticket on a steamship travelling by sea to the mouth of the Yukon, then up that long river to Dawson City. The trip from Seattle or Victoria could be made in three weeks, but space was very limited, since the few steamers that plied that route carried mostly freight; the trip included a stretch over open ocean that could be unpleasant; and the tickets were very expensive—well over $1,000 at the height of the rush. A much cheaper route was the tradi-

An underground view of mining activity on Bonanza Creek. Author's collection.

tional one over the Chilkoot or the White Pass, and this was the one that the majority of Klondikers took. There were other routes as well: the merchants of Edmonton, a small town at the end of the railroad in northern Alberta, touted an 'all-Canadian' route running from their community north to Lake Athabasca, thence to Great Slave Lake, down the Mackenzie to Fort McPherson, then to Alaska by way of the Rat, Bell, and Porcupine Rivers, and finally back up the Yukon River to Dawson City. A glance at a map should have discouraged anyone from trying it, yet over 1,600 people did, of whom roughly half succeeded in

reaching Dawson, though not until the spring of 1898. Several, including the police chief of Hamilton, Ontario, died en route of starvation and scurvy, trapped in the mountains between the Mackenzie Valley and Dawson City. It was this episode of misery and death that provided the inspiration for 'Klondike Days', Edmonton's annual summer festival.

Other routes were even less practical. Of the hundred Americans who tried to reach the Klondike by travelling across the Malaspina Glacier at the head of Yakutat Bay, nearly half died. The North-West Mounted Police tried an overland route from British Columbia to the Yukon by way

Government buildings and the Mounted Police barracks, Dawson City, 1898. Yukon Archives, Tappan Adney Collection, 81/9 G-29 #44.

of Fort Nelson, in the province's northeastern corner; it took them fourteen months. Others, including a party of Canadian soldiers sent to help the police preserve order in the Yukon, travelled through central British Columbia along the old telegraph trail to Teslin Lake and eventually the Klondike. Whatever the route, it was not an easy journey, except for the few who could afford ship passage up the Yukon River.

The great majority of Klondikers used the old route over one or other of the passes at the head of the Lynn Canal, where two towns a few kilometres apart, Skagway (serving the White Pass route) and Dyea (serving the more

popular Chilkoot Pass route), had sprung up to serve them. They landed at Skagway, by 1898 a city of 10,000 and a roaring frontier town in the lawless tradition of the American West. It was ruled by a gangster named Soapy Smith, whose agents robbed the 'cheechakos', as the greenhorns were called, or fleeced them in gambling dens. It is about 30 kilometres from tidewater to the Canadian border at the summit of the two passes, but it was a gauntlet that had to be run. Sam Steele, who commanded the Mounted Police in the Yukon at the height of the gold rush, described Skagway as it was when he saw the town early in 1898:

'O'Reilly Hall', a dance hall operated by the O'Reilly brothers on Bonanza Creek, decorated for Dominion Day, 1903. Mine workings can be seen on the extreme upper right. Author's collection.

Robbery and murder were daily occur-rences. . . . Shots were exchanged on the streets in broad daylight. . . . At night the crash of bands, shouts of 'Murder!' cries for help, mingled with the cracked voices of the singers in the variety halls; and the wily 'box rushers' [variety actresses] cheated the tenderfeet. . . . in the White Pass and above the town the shell game expert plied his trade, and occasionally some poor fellow was found lying lifeless on his sled where he had sat down to rest, the powder marks on his back, and his pockets inside out.[4]

In the summer of 1898, Soapy Smith met his fate in the great western tradition, shot dead by a vigilante, and Skagway settled down. The town was given a new lease on life when the White Pass and Yukon Railway linking it to White-horse was completed in 1900, and it now sur-vives, with a population of 750, as a destination for tens of thousands of tourists who come on summer cruise ships to see the spectacular coastline of British Columbia and Alaska.

On the map the Chilkoot Pass route looks easy enough. By a fluke of geography, the headwaters of the Yukon River lie at Lake Lindeman, less than 50 kilometres from the ocean at Dyea. From that lake it is possible to float or sail all the way to Dawson City, and past it roughly 1,500 kilometres to the Bering Strait, with only two impediments to navigation: the White Horse rapids and Miles Canyon, both near present-day Whitehorse. The hard part was getting to that lake. First the Klondikers walked from Skagway around a point of land to the smaller but equally corrupt town of Dyea. Nothing now remains of this community apart from a graveyard and a few rotting cabins, but it was lively enough in 1898. Here the Chilkoot trail started as an easy walk through spruce woods. Within two or three kilometres it began to steepen, however, and the small streams that crossed it, together with the scores of horses and people that used it, turned it to clinging mud.

In 25 kilometres a Klondiker would have climbed 300 metres and arrived at the community of Sheep Camp, a crude tent community where meals could be bought and packers hired to help carry goods over the pass. Now the trail became steeper still, and over the next 3 km it climbed to 600 m to reach 'the Scales', at the bottom of the pass itself. Here was the really difficult part, for the final stretch to the summit of the pass reached almost 1000 m in a short distance, and the last few hundred metres rose at an angle of nearly forty degrees.

Yet it was not the pass that made the experience such torture—it is used today by hikers, and is perhaps easier in winter, when most Klondikers went over it, than in summer, when large boulders uncovered by snow make walking more treacherous. What made the experience so grim was the number of times the pass had to be climbed. The Mounted Police, who guarded the Canadian border at the summit of the pass, decreed that no one would be permitted to cross it without enough money or supplies to last six months, which meant bringing perhaps a tonne of goods over the pass. If a man carried 45 kilograms—a heavy burden up a forty-degree slope—he would have to make the trip twenty times. The alternative was to hire Chilkat packers, who charged as much as two dollars a kilo, or use the aerial tramway that an ingenious entrepreneur had strung from the Scales to the summit; but this was also expensive. The famous images of men bent under massive packs, their heavy wool cold-weather gear wet with snow and sweat, climbing in lockstep up the slope—afraid to drop out lest they be forced to wait hours to get back in the queue—are all the more dramatic when one realizes that each one of them had to make the journey over and over again. It is no wonder that many Klondikers looked at the pass, sold their goods, at a loss, on the spot, and took the next ship home.

But thousands more did make the journey, and not all of them were men. Legend has it that the women who went to the Klondike were typically prostitutes, but this was not the case: like the miners, some were seeking wealth and some simply adventure. One of the best-known of this last group was Martha Black. Born in 1866, in Chicago, to a wealthy family, at the age of nineteen she married a railway executive. After a decade the two had become bored with middle-class life, and when they heard of the tonne of gold in Seattle, they decided to become Klondikers. But her husband had second thoughts about the Yukon and decided to go to Hawaii instead, so Martha left him and travelled north with only her brother as companion. She crossed the Chilkoot Pass in July 1898 and left a vivid account of the journey in her memoirs:

> In my memory it will ever remain a hideous nightmare. The trail led through a scrub pine forest where we tripped over bare roots of trees that curled over and around rocks and boulders like great devilfishes. Rocks! Rocks! Rocks! Tearing boots to pieces. Hands bleeding with scratches. I can bear it no longer. In my agony, I beg the men to leave me—to let me lie in my tracks.[5]

Of course they didn't leave her, and eventually she made it to Dawson City where she went into the lumber business, raised a son alone, and eventually married a local lawyer who had the luck and the political connections to become first the Territorial Commissioner and later the Yukon's member of Parliament. She served in Parliament herself while her husband was ill, becoming in 1935, at the age of 70, only the second woman elected to the House of Commons. She lived to be 91, and at her death in 1957 she was the undoubted doyenne of the Yukon. Her feelings about the Chilkoot Pass, like those of many others, were decidedly mixed. In her memoirs, first published in 1938 as *My Seventy Years*, she asked herself if she would do it again: 'Not for all the gold in the Klondyke' was the reply; 'And yet, knowing now what it meant, would I miss it? . . . No, never! . . . Not even for all the gold in the world!'

The alternative to the Chilkoot route was the White Pass, which was not so steep, cresting at just under 900 metres. It was, however, not only some 24 km longer, but wetter and hence muddier. For considerable periods it

Removing rock with a steam drill on Summit Cut during construction of the White Pass and Yukon Railway, *c.* 1899. NAC, PA182823.

was nearly impassable. But pack horses could be used along the entire trail, and hundreds of them broke their legs on it, or fell over cliffs, or died straining to the summit. A stretch of the trail named Dead Horse Gulch became infamous, and the American novelist Jack London wrote a horrifying description of the place:

> The horses died like mosquitoes in the first frost and from Skagway to Bennett they rotted in heaps. They died at the rocks, they were poisoned at the summit, and they starved at the lakes; they fell off the trail, what there was

Dawson City at midnight, 21 June 1899, looking south. The bridge to 'Lousetown', the red-light district, is visible at top centre. The houses extend much further up the 'Dome' than in the picture on the facing page, taken nearly a century later, and the government reserve is prominent in the centre. NAC, C20813.

of it, and they went through it; in the river they drowned under their loads or were smashed to pieces against the boulders; they snapped their legs in the crevices and broke their backs falling backwards with their packs; in the sloughs they sank from fright or smothered in the slime; and they were disembowelled in the bogs where the corduroy logs turned end up in the mud; men shot them, worked them to death and when they were gone, went back to the beach and bought more.[6]

It was the gentler grade of the White Pass that would lead the railroad builders to choose it over the Chilkoot, and thus to ensure the survival of Skagway.

Both the Chilkoot and the White Pass routes led to the same pair of joined lakes, Lindeman and Bennett. Here the Klondikers pitched camp and built boats from scratch by cutting trees and sawing the green lumber in saw-pits. These were platforms of rough logs with enough space between them to fit the tree to be sawn and a long straight saw with a han-

A modern view of Dawson City from the air. The Yukon River flows northwest out of top of the picture into Alaska. The
Klondike River flows in from the right, and the gold-bearing creeks are just to the right of the photographer's vantage
point. Across the Yukon River, the 'top of the world' highway heads towards Alaska. Yukon Government photo.

dle at both ends. One man stood on the ground and another on the platform, the first pulling on the saw and the second pushing. It was brutally hard work, and a fair division of labour was almost impossible. Many friendships and partnerships foundered before the boat was half-built. When, on 29 May 1898, the ice broke up on the lakes, 7,000 boats and rafts left for Dawson City. Five men were drowned in Miles Canyon before the Mounted Police began inspecting the vessels and forcing those judged unsafe to portage around the canyon—an entrepreneur built a crude tramway with logs for rails. But for most the trip to Dawson City was a pleasant one that involved no effort but steering.

By the time the first Klondikers reached Dawson City in the early summer of 1898, nearly two years after the discovery on Bonanza Creek, all the gold-bearing creeks had been staked and there were no more bonanzas to be found. Their choices were to turn around and go home—if they could afford to—or to find some sort of wage labour, either on some-

The river steamer *Whitehorse* entering the Five Fingers Rapids on the Yukon River, *c.* 1900. NAC, PA182826.

one else's claim or in Dawson City. By the end of that year the population of the Yukon had reached a number estimated at between thirty and forty thousand—nearly ten thousand more than it is today.

Dawson City at the height of the gold rush was a turbulent town, where gambling and prostitution were, if not legal, at least openly tolerated by the authorities. Saloons and dancehalls ran twenty-four hours a day, but, significantly, not seven days a week: they shut down at midnight on Saturday and remained closed until midnight on Sunday. This fact illustrates what in some ways was the most remarkable feature of the

Yukon during the gold rush—the power of the police to enforce a nominal orderliness on a community of considerable turbulence. However, theft and other property crimes were endemic.

The Yukon, made a District of the North-West Territories in July 1895 and a Territory in June 1898, was firmly under the control of the North-West Mounted Police. Local government consisted of the Territorial Commissioner and a small Council, all appointed by Ottawa rather than elected locally, and the council's meetings were at first closed to the public. The federal government was determined to have no hint of local self-government in the Yukon, so the laws were made and enforced by people who were in no way answerable to the population of the territory. These men—among them Sam Steele of the NWMP, who was also a member of the Council—had as their first priority the maintenance of public order. Although no proper census was taken in the Yukon until 1901, after the rush was over, there is no doubt that the population was overwhelmingly American. For this reason, the authorities were all the more determined that Dawson City would not become a wild-west town on the Skagway model, a development that might have cast doubt on Canadian sovereignty in the region.

Thus the government rushed police reinforcements to the Yukon. There had been 20 officers in the region when gold was discovered in 1896. By February 1898 they numbered 196, eventually reaching more than 300, and were backed up by the Yukon Field Force, a unit of 200 men drawn from the Canadian Army (nearly a quarter of the entire army!), who served in the Yukon from 1898 until 1900. The presence of 500 police and soldiers

Thousands of sacks of silver and lead concentrate from the Elsa-Keno mines awaiting shipment from Mayo to the south via river steamer and the Yukon and White Pass Railway, *c.* 1920. NAC, c21811.

in a population of at most 40,000 was one reason that Dawson was so free of violent crime. The other reason was that the Mounted Police were tireless in asserting their authority. They vigorously enforced the law against carrying weapons in Dawson City, and as a result there were very few murders in the Yukon during the rush, and none at all in the saloons—a notable contrast to the situation in Skagway. They enforced the peace in Dawson City partly by handing out stiff sentences—hard labour on the woodpile at the police barracks was the usual punishment for minor crimes—and since the commander of the police also served as magistrate, convictions were not difficult to obtain. The police made a habit of ordering bad characters to leave the Yukon, sometimes even when no real crime had been committed; this policy was very much in the tradition of the miners' meetings that the police had supplanted.

Of course, as the police themselves noted, the Yukon was not a good country for criminals. Not only was it hard to escape from the region unless one had highly developed survival skills, which most criminals did not, but there were only three common routes out, and the police guarded them all closely to make sure that the royalty on gold was paid. The fact

View of Whitehorse, c. 1900. It is early spring, and some river steamers wait to be launched on skids into the river. Others are already at the WP&YR sheds, taking on freight brought by the new railway from Skagway. Many residents are still living in tents. NAC, PA182825.

that anyone who tried to leave the Yukon overland took a serious risk of starving in the wilderness helped to curb violent impulses. The popular image of the Yukon, epitomized in Robert Service's famous poem 'The Shooting of Dan McGrew', is a product not of fact but of the idea that all frontiers must be violent, and of the popular confusion between the Yukon and the Alaskan mining communities, which did conform to the frontier stereotype.

Robert Service (1874–1958) was an Englishman who came to Canada at the age of 24 and, as an employee of the Canadian Bank of Commerce, was stationed for several years at Whitehorse and Dawson City. It was at Whitehorse, far from the events he recounted, that he wrote and published his first book of poems, *Songs of a Sourdough* (1907), which included 'Dan McGrew'. The first stanza sets the scene; its rough, forceful style shows why in his time he was called 'the Canadian Kipling':

A bunch of the boys were whooping it up in the Malamute saloon,
The kid that handles the music-box was hitting a jag-time tune;

Robert Service, the 'bard of the Klondike', in front of his Dawson City cabin in 1909. Author's collection.

Back of the bar, in a solo game, sat Dangerous
*   Dan McGrew*
And watching his luck was his light-o'love, the
*   lady that's known as Lou.*

As far as it goes, this is a reasonably accurate picture of saloon life in the gold-rush period. But then Service reaches for a dramatic climax:

Then I ducked my head, and the lights went
*   out, and two guns blazed in the dark;*
And a woman screamed, and the lights went
*   up, and two men lay stiff and stark;*
Pitched on his head, and pumped full of lead,
*   was Dangerous Dan McGrew,*

While the man from the creeks lay clutched to
*   the breast of the lady that's known as Lou.*

What is wrong with this picture is that there was not a single murder in a Dawson City saloon during the entire gold-rush period. The police did not permit men to carry firearms in town, and the law was strictly enforced. Since Service was writing eight years after the height of the rush, he may have been influenced by the tall tales told him by veterans. Or perhaps he just wanted to tell an exciting story. Of course this is popular verse, not a legal record of events. But Service was world-famous; he probably made more money from his work than any other poet writing in Canada, and there are still people who will declaim his verse at length unless forcibly prevented. For many, Service's work represents the truth of the gold rush, and it is a pity that he bent his material to fit preconceived ideas of what a 'frontier' society ought to be like. Presumably, though, a poem in which the climax consisted of an arrest for disorderly conduct, and the dénouement of a sentence to two weeks' work cutting stove wood, would not have had the same success.

The gold rush pushed the Canadian north onto the national and the world stage in a number of ways. The arrival of thirty to forty thousand people focused attention on the region, and public interest was heightened by the dispatches of the newspaper reporters who covered the story. The rush also forged important links between north and south. In order to improve the dismal communication links between the Territory and the outside, the federal government built a telegraph line to Dawson City. More impressive still was the construction, by a British consortium, of the White Pass and Yukon Railway, a narrow-gauge line built from Skagway through the White Pass to Whitehorse between 1898 and 1900, a distance of 166 kilometres. This was a remarkable feat of engineering, since the railroad had to climb from sea level to nearly 900 metres in just 33 km. Even more remarkable was the fact that the line was built without a cent of government subsidy; few North American railroads can make the same claim. Profitable from the beginning, the line operated for eighty years, and closed only when a downturn in the Yukon economy, and competition from a highway, put it out of business.

The section from Skagway to the Canadian border later reopened as a tourist attraction, however, and today provides a truly spectacular trip for the thousands who visit Skagway on cruise ships. For a few years the Yukon even had a second railway: in 1906 the Klondike Mines Railway was built from Dawson City to the creeks, using rolling stock shipped to the town by steamboat. But it never showed a profit, and closed in 1914.

The construction of the White Pass and Yukon Railway spurred the growth of the Yukon's second community, one that in time would supersede its rival to the north. The White Horse rapids marked the head of steamboat navigation on the Yukon River, and it was for that reason that the small settlement there was chosen as the terminus for the railroad. The town of Whitehorse flourished in summer as a transfer point between the trains and the boats, and in winter, on a much reduced scale, it handled passengers and mail transferring between the trains and the overland sled service to Dawson City.

The gold rush ended abruptly in the summer of 1899 when gold was discovered on the beaches of Nome, Alaska, and the more volatile elements of the population—those with the stamina to follow another rush—left the Yukon. The territory's population began a slow decline that was not reversed for forty years. The mining industry did not disappear, but its technology changed, and fewer people were needed in any case to extract the precious metal. If the rush itself had ended, however, the mines would remain profitable for several decades to come. In 1897 gold worth $2.5 million was taken from the creeks; in 1898 the value was $10 million; and in 1900, the year of greatest

A modern view of Carcross. The swing bridge has not been used since the railway ceased operations in the early 1980s. Yukon Government photo.

production, over $22 million. Total production up to 1911 amounted to $140 million—about $3.5 billion in modern Canadian dollars.

The Klondike gold rush was the first 'modern' event to occur in the Canadian North, in the sense that it brought to the region for the first time a large non-Native population, along with modern technology, urbanization, and all the other paraphernalia of the twentieth century. Though it left the NWT virtually untouched, it transformed the Yukon, or at least part of it; the Aboriginal people stood aside—or were excluded—from the events of the gold-rush period. The legacy of the 1890s for the Yukon was an infrastructure that, modern for its day, proceeded to decay over the next forty years; an economy dependent on world mineral prices; and a white population that shrank in twenty years from 40,000 to 2,500 and did not begin to grow again until the Second World War. The wealth of the North had always left the North, extracted by outsiders, and this was as true of the gold of the Yukon as it was of the furs and whales of the NWT.

The effect of the gold rush on the First Nations people of the North was not great. Although they were discriminated against by the mine owners, who would not hire them, it is not clear that many sought such work. Some did take seasonal wage employment cutting wood or in other similar occupations, but most continued doing what their people had done since the arrival of the Hudson's Bay Company sixty years earlier: supplementing their traditional economy with the small cash income provided by trapping for furs. The gold rush transformed part of the Yukon, but the part that was still the preserve of the Native people was to remain largely unaltered for another half-century.

CHAPTER SEVEN

Quiet Years, 1900-1940

At the beginning of the twentieth century development in the Canadian North was dramatically uneven. In the far west, the Yukon had become a separate territory, with a population that the 1901 census reported as 27,000, of whom 9,000 lived in Dawson City. It boasted a telephone and electric power system (in Dawson City), two railways, telegraph links with the outside world, and an active and profitable industrial sector. Though the Yukon and NWT were both territories, lying in the same latitudes, some aspects of their history were so different between 1900 and 1950 that they might as well have been on different continents. The Yukon was a part, albeit a distant and declining one, of the Canadian and world economies as they existed in that period. The rest of the North-West Territories north of the 60th parallel, by contrast, had hardly been touched at all by the world developments of the nineteenth century, let alone of the early twentieth. The non-Native population of that huge region consisted of a handful of fur traders and missionaries; what the Native population was, no one knew, since in 1900 there were still a good many Inuit in the central

Arctic who had not been contacted by outsiders, let alone counted by them.

These years saw the modern Northwest Territories assume their present boundaries. In 1905 the provinces of Alberta and Saskatchewan were created out of the old North-West Territories, with their northern boundaries set, like British Columbia's, at the 60th parallel. In 1912 Manitoba's boundaries were extended to the same limit, and in the same year the northern boundary of Quebec was pushed even farther north, to the tip of the Ungava peninsula. While the southern sections of the NWT were being carved away, new land was being added in the high Arctic, for it was in this same period that the last major islands of the Arctic archipelago where being charted—the islands discovered at the turn of the century by Otto Sverdrup and named for him, and later Borden and Meighen Islands, discovered by Vilhjalmur Stefansson during the Canadian Arctic Expedition of 1914–18. When the last bits of land were mapped after the Second World War (Prince Charles Island in Foxe Basin, quite a sizeable piece of land at 130 by 100 kilometres, was

Hydraulic mining at Lovett Gulch, Yukon, in 1911. The technique was not kind to the environment. Author's collection.

found as late as 1948 by an RCAF aerial survey), what was left of the NWT was the largest political unit in the country, amounting to 3.38 million km², or 34 per cent of Canada. The Yukon, at 482,000 km², made up just under 5 per cent.

Although the Yukon had reached a far more advanced level of economic development than the rest of the North, in 1900 its population was beginning a forty-year decline. There was still plenty of gold in the region, but it was not concentrated, and the old labour-intensive methods of production would no longer pay. The first change was to hydraulic mining, which involved melting and stripping the gravel not with fires, which were inefficient and had denuded the Dawson City region of timber, but by high-pressure hoses that dissolved the creek beds and made sluicing on a large scale possible. To produce the necessary pressure and flow of water, a water ditch over 110 kilometres long was built to bring water to Bonanza Creek through a system of ditch, flume, pipe, and inverted siphon. A bridge still standing across the Klondike River and massive sections of cast-iron pipe rusting beside it in the weeds bear witness to this remarkable project. Equally visible is the spectacular damage that such unregulated operations did to the Klondike environment.

Dredge tailings near Dawson City, 1922, looking south. The Klondike River flows across the picture from left to
right, and Bonanza Creek flows in from the top. The buildings were used by the Yukon Consolidated Gold
Company until 1964, and are now open to tourists. NAC, PA164036.

This kind of mining could not be carried on without large infusions of capital. In the years after 1900, individual miners sold their claims, or let them lapse, and capitalists moved in to take them over. The Guggenheims, A.N.C. Treadgold, and 'Klondike Joe' Boyle all raised capital and went into large-scale mining. The final stage of gold mining for these companies, known locally as 'concessions' because of the special arrangements they had with the federal government, was the use of dredges. These were huge, expensive machines that floated on the creeks. At the front of each one was a large

boom with an endless chain of buckets that chewed the creek beds to a depth of up to 12 metres. Inside the dredge the gold was extracted by a more sophisticated version of the sluice box; then the residue was carried out the back on a conveyor belt along a boom that moved from side to side, depositing the tailings in the serpentine piles of gravel and round stones that are still a notable feature of the lower Klondike River valley. Powered by hydro-electricity, the dredges were floated up the creeks on lakes that they made themselves; a dam was built behind the dredge and the creek

Cominco Mine, Yellowknife, 1937. NWT Archives, Maranda Collection, N91-032:0005.

bed was allowed to fill with enough water to float it; then it worked itself along the creek, taking the lake with it.

These dredges were expensive: Joe Boyle built one in 1910 that cost $300,000. But they moved such quantities of gravel that they could make a profit from material that had only a few cents' worth of gold in a cubic metre. Operating from May to November, they kept the gold industry going until 1964, when the Yukon Consolidated Gold Company's last machine shut down and large-scale gold mining in the Yukon ceased, probably for ever. The last dredge has been restored by Parks Canada, however, and the gold company's offices and workshops remain, untouched since 1964 and virtually unchanged since 1910, for the public to visit. There is still considerable gold pro-

duction in the Yukon today, but it is carried on, as it was in 1897, by individual claim-holders; and although they use hydraulic methods, they now operate under strict environmental regulations. The amount of activity depends on the price of gold; when it reached $800 Canadian per ounce in the early 1980s there was a flurry of activity, but today only a few part-time miners work the creeks.

Gold was not the Yukon's only profitable mineral. There are extensive and rich copper deposits near Whitehorse, which were first exploited in 1900. But with copper, as with so much else in the Yukon, the great expense was transportation, and mining copper there paid only when world prices were high, as they were in 1906 and during the First World War. In 1916, 1.25 million kilograms of copper ore were shipped from the Yukon, but prices fell after the war, and in 1920 operations ceased, not to be revived for another forty years. There were also rich deposits of silver, lead, and zinc in the Stewart River region, and an active mining community grew up centred on the Yukon River community of Mayo. But, then as now, mineral production, on which so much of the Yukon's prosperity was based, was entirely dependent on fluctuations in world prices, and the high cost of transportation made it vulnerable to downturns.

The conversion of gold mining to hydraulic and dredging operations required many fewer workers than the old methods had, and since no new bonanzas were found after 1900, the population of the Yukon shrank steadily throughout the first two decades of the twentieth century. Between 1901 and 1911 it dropped by more than half, to just over 8,000, and by 1921 it had been halved again, hitting a low point in that year of 4,127, of whom about 1,500 were Native people. It took only 2,500 non-Native Yukoners to run the gold and other mining operations that year, along with the steamboats and all the other commercial and service operations of the territory.

The Native people of the Yukon had not been affected in any profound way by the turbulent events of the gold rush. Although the rush had in a sense transformed the territory, the area actually touched by it—mostly the Klondike region and the Yukon River corridor—was very small. Indians were discriminated against in hiring, and almost none worked in mining on the creeks. This was not employment that would have suited them in any case, since most preferred to keep the way of life they had followed for nearly a century,

supplementing the living they made from the land with participation in the fur trade. Those who sought employment for wages usually took jobs that permitted intermittent labour, such as cutting cord wood for the steamboats on the Yukon River. In this as in other things, the Native people took what they needed from the new economic order and used it to their own advantage. It is true, however, that the gold rush saw a decline in their numbers, presumably through introduced diseases. Though exact figures are not available, in 1921 the Native population of the Yukon was probably 20 or 30 per cent of what it had been in the same general area a century earlier. However depleted their numbers, though, the First Nations of the Yukon continued to follow their own way of life. It was not until the advent of the social welfare state after the Second World War that their lives would be affected in any dramatic way by outsiders.

In 1921 the Yukon's population fell to a historic low point, and twenty years later it had risen very little. The Territory had reached a kind of stasis, with a white population made up of a small cadre of administrators, some missionaries and traders, and those who worked for the transportation and mining industry. The Native population was also stable, its higher birth rate balanced by a higher mortality.

In the Northwest Territories, the intrusion on the way of life of the Native people ranged from slight, in the Mackenzie River Valley, to none at all in the central Arctic and Foxe Basin region. The main outside force was the fur trade, dominated by the Hudson's Bay Company, with Revillon Frères and independent traders also taking a share. A handful of missionaries and the occasional explorer (this last

The first bank in the NWT, at Fort Smith, 1922. NWT Archives, Jackson Collection, N79-004:0161.

category was non-resident, of course) made up the balance of the non-Native population. Nevertheless, the beginning of the twentieth century saw the first signs of concern on the part of the federal government to protect its interests in the region.

Canada had acquired the continental part of the NWT with the transfer of Rupert's Land from the Hudson's Bay Company in 1870, and in 1880 Britain had transferred the islands of the Arctic archipelago to the country. But Canada's title to portions of this vast territory was tenuous, as Britain's had been, particularly in the high Arctic, where much of the land was unoccupied and had been discovered,

explored, and in some cases claimed by citizens of other countries. For the first thirty years after Confederation, Canada virtually ignored its holdings north of the 60th parallel. The country had a small population, limited resources, and more important tasks to accomplish: in particular, bringing other provinces into the union and building the first transcontinental railway. Prior to the arrival of the first party of Mounted Police in the Yukon in 1894, Ottawa's assertion of its rights in the territories consisted of two summer voyages to the eastern Arctic to build cairns and wave flags, but there had been no concrete or permanent display of sovereign right. Canadian sovereignty

Prospector's cabin at Yellowknife. NAC, PA101737.

in the North was unchallenged not because it was indisputable—it rested on very shaky ground, particularly where the Arctic islands were concerned—but simply because no other country was interested in challenging it.

The first intrusion of government into the NWT occurred in the summer of 1899, when the Dene of the upper Mackenzie River Valley signed Treaty 8. This treaty, the majority of whose signatories lived in what was soon to become northern Alberta, was proposed by the government to establish the rights of the region's First Nations in the face of the initial encroachment of white hunters and trappers onto their traditional lands and especially the

intrusion of the hundreds of would-be Klondikers who had passed through this region on their way to the Yukon. The government's policy in such matters was not to offer a treaty unless there was a possibility of such encroachment. Believing that white intrusion was less likely north of the Treaty 8 region, the government felt that the Dene there would, in the words of Frank Oliver, minister of the Interior from 1905 to 1911, be 'best left as Indians'.[1] It was not until 1921, in the wake of the discovery of oil at Norman Wells, that the government brought Treaty 11 to the Dene of the central and lower Mackenzie Valley, thus introducing a government presence to the

Pauline Cove at Herschel Island is the best natural harbour in the region, and thus became the centre of the western Arctic whaling fleet. The terrain is so flat that it is difficult to get an impression of the scale, but the two-masted ship at right centre gives an idea. RCMP photo 4085-1.

western NWT. The treaty, however, was never fully implemented; in particular, the promised reserves were never set up.

In 1903, two small but significant incursions into the north were made by the North-West Mounted Police (after 1904 the Royal North-West Mounted Police; after 1920 the Royal Canadian Mounted Police). Both were demonstrations of sovereignty; after the success of the effort to regulate society during the gold rush, the government was emboldened to assert its authority in even more remote places.

Just off the Yukon's Arctic coast, not far east of the 141st meridian, where the Yukon–Alaska boundary completes its long journey to the Beaufort Sea, lies a flat, treeless island about 10 by 12 kilometres in area. The only distinguishing feature of Herschel Island is that it has the best harbour in the long stretch of Arctic coast between Point Barrow and the Mackenzie Delta. Beginning in 1889, it was used as a wintering harbour for the ships of the western Arctic whaling fleet. These ships represented the last flourishing of the north Pacific whaling industry, which by the late nineteenth century had exterminated most of the animals south of the Arctic circle. By the 1880s, American whaling ships were pressing

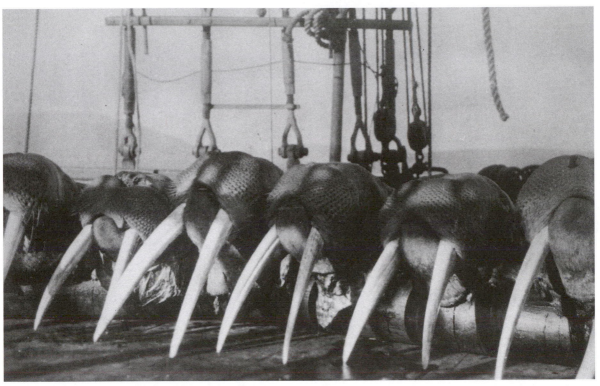

Heads of walrus killed at Chesterfield Inlet, *c.* 1926. NWT Archives, Learmonth Collection, N87-033:0214.

north into Bering Strait, and in 1888 one enterprising captain discovered that there were large numbers of bowhead whales—'thick as bees',[2] the report said—to the east of Point Barrow, the northernmost tip of Alaska.

Despite the development of petroleum products and the invention of synthetic materials such as celluloid and bakelite, there was still a good market for the products of the whale hunt at the turn of the century. In 1900 the price of whale oil was $15 a barrel in San Francisco, and baleen (the cartilage-like substance that hangs in the whale's mouth to filter out food; tough yet flexible, it was used for corset stays) brought $12 a kilogram. A good-sized bowhead whale yielded a hundred barrels of oil and a thousand kilos of baleen, making it worth up to $13,500.

Whaling ships operating in the Beaufort Sea almost always wintered at Herschel Island because the navigation season was so short, and the distance from the home port, usually San Francisco, so long, that it was impractical to make a round trip each year. In 1890 two ships wintered at Pauline Cove, as the island's harbour was christened. One of them, the *Mary D. Hume*, returned home the next summer after a two-year absence with a cargo worth $400,000—the most profitable voyage in the history of American whaling. Returns of this magnitude acted as a magnet. During the winter of 1894–95 fifteen ships sheltered at

Buildings on Herschel Island at the end of the whaling era, around 1910. RCMP photo 4071-13.

Herschel Island, and the next year it was reported that twelve hundred people were living there, some on the ships and others in quite substantial buildings constructed on the island.

This situation had disquieting implications for Canadian sovereignty in the north. The whalers did just as they pleased at Herschel Island and in the Beaufort Sea, for until 1894 there was no agent of the Canadian government within 1,500 kilometres of the region; even after the NWMP arrived in the Klondike they were still hundreds of impassable kilometres away from Herschel Island, and had no effect on the whalers' operations. The whalers hired Inuit hunters to get meat for them and Inuit women to cook, sew, and clean, and in some cases the ships' officers took the women as mistresses, an arrangement (forbidden to the ship's crews) that gave the women status among their people.

The difficulty for the Canadian government was twofold. First, reports from Herschel Island suggested that the whalers were debauching the Inuit, both in their sexual relationships and in teaching them to make—and consume—a home-brew based on raisins and molasses. Second, the amount of trade was considerable: between 1891 and 1907, when the industry had all but ceased, 1,345 whales were taken in the Beaufort Sea, worth nearly $13.5 million, while another $1.4 million had been made through trade with the Inuit. No royalties or tariffs had been paid on any of this money, and although the whalers had no interest in making territorial claims in the region, the fact that they were operating in a no-man's land cast doubt on Canada's rights in the region.

The nature and amount of the harm done to the Inuit by the whalers is debatable. The missionaries and the Mounted Police (who got the reports at second hand when they filtered down to Dawson City) were inclined to believe the worst. Inspector Charles Constantine reported in 1895 that

> *the carryings-on of the officers and crews of the whalers there was such that no one would believe. . . . large quantities of whiskey are taken up in the ships.'. . . as long as the liquor lasts, the natives neither fish nor hunt, and die of starvation in consequence. . . . The captains and mates of these vessels purchase for their own use girls from nine years and upwards.*[3]

What the Inuit themselves thought is impossible to say. However, the Inuit hunter Nuligak, a small boy at the time the whalers were at Herschel Island, in his old age dictated his memoirs of the era. He describes his first meeting with the whalers in 1902, the year before the arrival of the police:

> *When summer came Uncle Kralogark took us west to Herschel Island. . . . Crowds of Eskimos came there. That fall I saw some very large ships. The sailors we met always had something in their mouths, something they chewed. It so intrigued me that I kept staring at their jaws. One certain day that 'thing' was given to me. I chewed—it was delicious. It was chewing gum. From that day I was able to recognize some of these white men's things.*[4]

Among his happiest memories were the Christmas celebrations put on by the newcomers. However, in the forty years after 1890 so many Inuit of the Mackenzie Delta region died of disease that the population was nearly wiped out (the present inhabitants moved in to replace them). This suggests that the presence of the whalers was indeed fatal.

Demands for government action began in 1893 with the arrival of the first missionary on the island. Isaac O. Stringer, a twenty-seven-year-old Anglican priest, had just graduated from Wycliffe College in Toronto. Later bishop of the Yukon and famous as 'The Bishop Who Ate His Boots' (the title of his biography; once, lost in the wilderness, he had boiled and eaten his boots to keep from starving), he was apprehensive about meeting the whalers, but to his relief they made him welcome. He adopted a cautious policy towards the whalers' relations with the Inuit, and his one sermon on the evils of drink gave no offence; perhaps it was not intended to. Stringer was well aware of the ambivalent nature of his situation, writing of his dilemma:

> *I could not have been much better used under the circumstances if I had been the President of the United States. But I can't help but feel that a little indiscretion on my part or some undue circumstances might cause just as hearty an opposition. Why should they be friendly to a lonely missionary, who, if he says all he thinks, would condemn some of their darling sins? . . . I know that many of them would do a great deal for me or anyone else in my place under the circumstances in this country. But this winter I got a better insight into their life and manner of living. . . .*[5]

In 1897 Stringer brought his wife, Sadie, to the island, and two of their children were born

Cutting the head of a bowhead whale, Pangnirtung, 1946. HBC Archives, N79-189.

there. When they left in 1901 they were replaced by another missionary, C.E. Whittaker.

Despite appeals from the Anglican Church, the federal government hesitated to send a government agent to the region. The Mounted Police were the obvious candidates for the job, but they were preoccupied with the gold rush, and thus it was not until the rush was over that a detachment could be spared for the western Arctic. In the summer of 1903, however, a party consisting of Superintendent Charles Constantine, who had served in the Yukon, Sergeant F.J. Fitzgerald, and four constables was sent down the Mackenzie River to establish one detachment at Fort McPherson and another on Herschel

Island. The Herschel Island detachment, consisting of Sergeant Fitzgerald and Constable F.D. Sutherland, was set up in August of that year. The two men travelled to their new post from the Mackenzie Delta in a boat borrowed from the Anglican missionary.

The establishment of the Mounted Police detachment on Herschel Island was typical of the hasty planning and threadbare provisioning that marked government operations in the North at the time. Fitzgerald and Sutherland were sent to that remote spot with inadequate supplies and no arrangements for housing. They had to spend their first winter in a sod house borrowed from one of the whaling companies, warming themselves with coal also borrowed from the company. Though they could and did enforce the law on the island, particularly the customs regulations, their real control over events was minimal. The actual hunting of whales and trading with the Inuit took place in the Beaufort Sea and along the Arctic coast, not on the island, and because the police did not have a boat, they could not supervise what was going on. They were reduced to asking the whaling captains what goods they had traded with the Inuit and charging them customs duties accordingly. For the same reason their attempts to enforce prohibitions on selling or giving liquor to the Inuit did not succeed.

But actual enforcement of laws and regulations was not the real purpose of the Herschel Island detachment. Rather, it was a demonstration of Canadian sovereignty over the region. Although the whaling industry was dead by 1914, Herschel Island continued to be a centre for the fur trade, and in 1915 the Hudson's Bay Company opened a post there. But this trade in turn declined, and in the 1930s the economic centre of the western Arctic shifted to the Mackenzie Delta community of Aklavik. By 1940 the island was deserted. It was not until the oil boom of the 1970s that attention was again focused on it, this time in connection with the debate over the exploitation of the petroleum resources of the region. In 1987 Herschel Island was made a Territorial Park, the Yukon's first.

The second incursion into the Northwest Territories, also in 1903, was, like the first, aimed at controlling foreign whalers. The northeastern part of the North had its own whaling industry. Here there were two fleets: one from Scotland that operated in Baffin Bay

Inspector F.J. Fitzgerald (1869–1911), of 'Lost Patrol' fame.
RCMP photo 2394.

during the summer, returning home each fall, and an American fleet that operated in Hudson Bay, wintering at Cape Fullerton on the northwest coast. There were fewer ships in Hudson Bay than in the Beaufort Sea, and the industry had been operating longer, but in 1903 the government chartered the *Neptune*, a Newfoundland sealing schooner, and dispatched a Mounted Police detachment to Cape Fullerton under the command of Superintendent J.D. Moodie. As at Herschel Island, the authorities had mixed success in controlling the whalers. They did enforce a ban on shooting musk-oxen, which were being extensively hunted for their

Captain J.-E. Bernier (1852–1934) holding a trophy, *c.* 1923. Bernier led a number of seagoing expeditions to the Arctic on behalf of the Canadian government between 1904 and 1925. NAC, PA101850.

hides, but their effect on whaling and trading with the Inuit of the region was not great.

In the early years of this century, the government sent several expeditions to the Arctic under the command of J.-E. Bernier (1852–1934), Canada's most experienced mariner, to demonstrate sovereignty and to collect customs duties from whalers and traders. In the summer of 1911 Bernier set up a plaque on Melville Island officially claiming the Arctic archipelago for Canada. The Mounted Police were sent even farther afield in the 1920s,

when detachments were set up at a number of very remote places in the eastern and high Arctic: on Baffin Island at Pond Inlet (1922), Pangnirtung (1923), and Lake Harbour (1927); on Devon Island at Dundas Harbour (1924); and on Ellesmere Island at Craig Harbour (1922) and Bache Peninsula (1926).

The last of these detachments, which operated for seven years, illustrates the manner in which the Canadian government demonstrated its rather shaky claim to sovereignty over the archipelago of the high Arctic. The post was located on the east coast of Ellesmere Island, just north of the 79th parallel. Except for the Greenland Inuit at Etah, who fell outside the jurisdiction of the police, there were no human inhabitants within hundreds of kilometres: just two members of the Mounted Police and a few Inuit employees. The purpose of this detachment was not to exercise the ordinary functions of the police, but to fly the Canadian flag over a region of which a large portion had been discovered by nationals of non-British countries. It was for this reason that the police ran a post office at Bache Peninsula. Mail was delivered once a year, in August, when the annual supply ship arrived (except for the occasional year when the ice was bad; then supplies and mail were left on the ice some distance south of the post). A once-a-year post office may well seem absurd, but operating a postal service is the sort of administrative function that is clear evidence of a nation's sovereignty over a particular territory. It was for this reason that the police stamped the outgoing letters; in fact, this was the only reason the police were there.

A number of dramatic incidents brought the western Arctic to national attention in the

Cutting and rendering whale blubber, Pangnirtung, 1937. HBC Archives, N8124.

early decades of this century. The first was the 'Lost Patrol' of 1910–11. Normally, the Royal North-West Mounted Police carried mail and instructions to Fort McPherson in the winter by means of a sled patrol from Dawson City. But in December 1910 this annual patrol set out the other way round, from Fort McPherson, headed by F.J. Fitzgerald, a veteran of northern service and by then an inspector in the force. Trying to find the pass in the mountains between the two communities, the patrol, consisting of Fitzgerald, two constables, and an ex-constable acting as guide, lost their way. Instead of admitting defeat and

retracing their steps, they used up many days and most of their food in vain attempts to find the right path. Trapped by bad weather—on one day the temperature reached -53C with a strong wind—they ate their dogs, and then they died, three of starvation and one by suicide. The episode is particularly poignant because of Fitzgerald's personal circumstances, though all the facts were not known at the time. He had served at Herschel Island for seven years, with only occasional leaves in the south, and had married an Inuit woman 'after the fashion of the country'. When he applied to the force for permission to marry her legal-

The Dempster patrol preparing to leave Dawson City to search for Fitzgerald and his party, early 1911. Yukon Archives, 82/336 H-45.

ly, his superior officer refused, saying he would rather hear that Fitzgerald had shot himself than that he had married a Native woman. As a result the two did not marry, but they did have a daughter who was crippled in a childhood accident, attended a residential school in Hay River in the 1920s (the RCMP contributed informally to her maintenance), and died in her teens. Despite his unwelcome marriage request, Fitzgerald's reputation in the force was high, and when he died he was on his way south to take command of the police contingent travelling to London to attend the coronation of King George V; at the same time he

was to marry a young American woman he had met during his previous leave. The police were criticized for risking lives in order to set a speed record, a charge that was probably true—Fitzgerald was travelling with much less than the usual supply of food—and therefore stung badly.

Three other incidents are less well known now, though they created a considerable stir at the time. In June 1912 two explorers, the American H.V. Radford and the Canadian George Street, were murdered by their Inuit guides near the southern end of Bathurst Inlet, apparently because Radford had lost his temper and struck one of the men. The investigation of this case involved a series of patrols that lasted from the summer of 1914 until the early months of 1918, when the killers were found and questioned, but not charged; it was felt that they had been provoked, and that it would be wrong to punish them since they had no idea of Canadian law. Then, late in 1913, two Oblate missionary priests, Fathers Rouvière and Le Roux, were killed by Sinnisiak and Uluksuk, their Inuit guides, near Bloody Falls on the Coppermine River, because one of the priests had threatened one of the Inuit. This time the Mounted Police arrested the men involved, in the summer of 1916, and brought them to Alberta for trial. To the chagrin of the police, and of the Roman Catholic Church, the trial for the murder of Father Rouvière, which was held in Edmonton in the summer of 1917, resulted in an acquittal. The two men were taken to Calgary, tried again for the murder of Father Le Roux, and were convicted, but were given a short sentence of detention at the police detachment at Fort Resolution, and were soon returned to their people. The statement of Sinnisiak showed how cultural misunderstanding in the North could lead to tragedy:

Sinnisiak and Uluksuk, killers of Fathers Rouvière and Le Roux, photographed after their arrest in 1916. RCMP photo 4566-3.

Ilogoak [Le Roux] was carrying a rifle. He was mad with us when we started back from their camp and I could not understand his talk. I asked Ilogoak if he was going to kill me and he nodded his head. . . . he pushed me again and wanted me to put on the harness and then he took his rifle out on top of the sled. I was very scared and started to pull. We went a little way and Uluksuk and I started to talk and Ilogoak put his hand over my mouth.

Ilogoak was very mad and was pushing me. I was thinking hard and crying and very scared and the frost was in my boots and I was cold. I wanted to go back. I was afraid. Ilogoak would not let us. Every time the sled stuck Ilogoak would pull out the rifle. I got hot inside my body. . . . I was very much afraid. . . . he looked away from me and I stabbed him in the back with a knife.[6]

In April 1922 another murder of this type took place in the North, when an Inuk named Alikomiak shot and killed Corporal W.A. Doak of the Mounted Police while under arrest for the murder of a trader. The event aroused a good deal of public interest, and there was a strong feeling in the government that the perpetrator should be made an example. Accordingly, Alikomiak, along with other Inuit charged with various crimes, was taken to the police detachment at Herschel Island for trial, the judge, prosecutor, and defence attorney travelling the long distance from Edmonton for the event. Alikomiak and Tatimagana were convicted of murder, and on 1 February 1924 they were hanged at Herschel Island, the first Inuit to be executed under Canadian law. The episode was strong proof of the Canadian government's determination to see its writ run as far as the Arctic Ocean.

Another dramatic episode revolved around Albert Johnson, the 'mad trapper' of Rat River, and took place in the winter of 1931–32. Johnson (probably not his real name) was a white trapper living in the lower Mackenzie Valley, near Fort McPherson. Apparently he had become 'bushed' and had interfered with the traplines of the local Dene population. When they complained to the RCMP and the police went to investigate, Johnson shot at them. A midwinter chase ensued, with four separate patrols sent out to apprehend the trapper, but he was so skilled at survival that it was not until a radio-equipped airplane was called in that the police managed to track him down. The episode ended with one police officer dead, another officer and a member of the Canadian Army Signal Corps badly wounded, and Johnson himself shot, possibly a suicide. It

was rough evidence of what northern conditions could do to an unstable mind, and wonderful fodder for the newspapers.

Although all these incidents were well publicized at the time, the only story that has lingered in the popular memory is that of the 'mad trapper', probably because his identity has never been conclusively established. The others were quickly forgotten by outsiders, and eventually faded even from the collective memory of northerners. In fact, that collective memory was typically short, and the reason was that the non-Native society of the North was so transient. Those who came north to exploit a frontier, not to establish a homeland, had their hearts and memories rooted elsewhere, in their real homes in the south. The best illustration of the North's short memory is the story of the sinking of the *Princess Sophia*, the single most spectacular tragedy in the history of the modern North, which took place at the end of the First World War.

The *Princess Sophia* was a passenger and freight steamship owned by a subsidiary of the Canadian Pacific Railway Company. Built in Scotland in 1911, the ship was 74.5 metres long and capable of carrying between 250 and 500 passengers, depending on how she was fitted out. Arriving in Vancouver in 1912, she was immediately put into service on the run between Seattle, Vancouver, and Skagway. This route was the means of exit for the entire population of the Yukon River Valley, both in the Yukon and far down the river into Alaska. Residents of Fairbanks and the mining communities of Alaska who wanted to travel south took a river steamer upstream past the 141st meridian into Canada, past Dawson City to Whitehorse, where they boarded the train to Skagway

Inuit grave, 1935. NAC, PA99563.

and then a ship to Vancouver or Seattle. It was a long trip, but it was the quickest and easiest way south, and many hundreds of northerners preferred to make it every year, rather than endure six months of a northern winter.

On 23 October 1918, the *Princess Sophia* left Skagway with 354 passengers and crew. This was a greater load than usual, but freeze-up was starting on the Yukon River, shutting down the river steamers, and anyone who wanted to leave the North had to do so by the end of October. Steaming south down the Lynn Canal at night in a snowstorm, the ship went off course and ran up on Vanderbilt Reef, a low rocky ledge about 50 kilometres north of Juneau. The Inside Passage can be treacherous; as this is being written, the *Star Princess*, a luxury cruise ship, has run aground on Poundstone Rock, only 8 km south of where the *Princess Sophia* came to grief; the modern mishap has apparently caused no injuries, except to the reputations of her navigators. The *Sophia*, on the other hand, sat high and apparently safe on Vanderbilt Reef for a day and a half, while her captain, Leonard Locke, waited for the wind to drop so that the passengers could be safely transferred to a flotilla of fishing boats that had come out from Juneau to help. But the wind did not drop; the weather worsened, the fishing boats ran for cover, and in the early evening of 25 October the wind and waves lifted the ship, pivoted her around on the reef, and pushed her across it, tearing the hull and sinking her stern-first. Some of the passengers and crew tried to launch the lifeboats, but they were swamped; others jumped into the water, but the temperature was at freezing, and they suffocated in the thick bunker oil that coated the surface. There were no survivors; 354 men, women, and children were killed.

This was an almost unthinkable disaster for the Yukon River Valley; approximately eight per cent of the non-Native population of the Yukon went down with the *Princess Sophia*. Yet the remaining population was so transient, and so firmly rooted in the south, that the incident left no permanent marks in the Yukon. All the bodies that were recovered were buried in Juneau or in southern locations; not one was returned to the North for burial, and although there are gravestones in Vancouver, Victoria, and other southern cities that speak of the *Sophia*, there are no memorials in Dawson City, Fairbanks, or anywhere else in the North. It was the worst maritime disaster in the history of the north Pacific coast—the region's version of the *Titanic*—yet except among marine enthusiasts it is almost unknown.

In this era, the foundations of the northern economy continued to be mining and fur trading. In 1921 the Yukon and Northwest Territories produced minerals worth $1.7 million and $2 million in furs; in 1931 the totals were $2.2 million and $2.1 million. But the

stability that these figures imply is deceptive, for although the prices of minerals, particularly gold, did not change much in this period, the prices of furs changed dramatically from year to year, depending on supply and the dictates of world fashion. In the early 1920s, when silver-fox pelts were much in demand, some Inuit trappers along the Arctic coast were reported to have made $10,000 in a season, a fortune for those days. But the demand dropped, and with the onset of the great depression of the 1930s it collapsed.

The high prices of the early 1920s had brought increased competition to the region, with the Alberta-based Northern Trading Company and Lamson and Hubbard operating in the Mackenzie region, and the French firm of Revillon Frères in Keewatin. But the wild swings in price proved too much for these smaller concerns, and by the outbreak of the Second World War Revillon Frères had sold out to the Hudson's Bay Company, leaving the old firm dominant in the North.

In the inter-war years, two important mining centres were developed to challenge the Klondike—declining, though still productive—as the mineral capital of the Canadian North. One was in a remote region of the northern Canadian Shield, at the southeastern corner of Great Bear Lake. Here, in 1930, a mining promoter and prospector named Gilbert Labine (1890–1977) discovered a rich deposit of silver mixed with pitchblende, the mineral from which radium is extracted. In 1932, the worst year of the Depression, 300 men converged on the region to stake claims. Used in medicine to treat cancer, and on instrument dials, radium was far more valuable than gold, and even the small amounts

S. SOPHIA ON VANDERBILT REEF — WINTER ᵀ POND ©

The *Princess Sophia* fast aground on Vanderbilt Reef, 24 October 1918. She sank the next day with a loss of 354 lives. Alaska State Library, PCA 87-1702.

found in Labine's ore samples were valued by the assayer at $8,000 per tonne. This tremendous value permitted Labine to form a company named Eldorado, which built not only a mine and concentrating plant at Port Radium but the transportation system that took the concentrate by river to Waterways and the railhead in Alberta, from where it was taken to an extraction plant at Port Hope, near Toronto. Although competition cut the price so much that Port Radium was mothballed by 1939, the war raised prices again, and the mine was briefly reopened.

A more lasting mining centre, developed at about the same time, was located at Yellowknife, on the north arm of Great Slave Lake. Prospectors travelling to the radium finds to the north found traces of gold in Yellowknife Bay, and claims were staked beginning in 1934. In 1938, 3,500 claims were registered, and eventually three major gold mines went into production. Between 1938, when the first gold was produced, and 1942, when the mines were temporarily closed by the war, the Yellowknife region produced 366,000 ounces of gold, worth over $10 million; the same amount would be worth $183 million today.

This was the era in which aviation really

came into its own in the North, the great age of the bush pilot. The difference between travelling into the North for weeks by foot and canoe and doing so in a few hours by airplane can hardly be overestimated, and remote communities such as the one at Port Radium could hardly have existed without the new technology. The relationship between the northern mining boom of the inter-war period and the fledgling airline companies was a symbiotic one; the planes made the mines possible, and the mines gave the companies the business that fuelled their early growth.

The two most famous Canadian bush pilots were W.R. 'Wop' May (1896–1952) and Grant McConachie (1909–65). As a young pilot on the western front, in 1918 May had narrowly escaped being shot down by the famous 'Red Baron'. He went on to become Canada's leading northern pilot in the 1920s, and achieved international fame when he provided aerial transportation and reconnaissance for the Mounted Police party who pursued and killed the 'mad trapper' of Rat River in 1932. Grant McConachie began an airmail and freight service between Edmonton and the Yukon in 1933, did extensive air exploration in the early stages of the Alaska Highway and Canol projects, and eventually sold his company to Canadian Pacific Airlines, of which he became president in 1947.

There were many other bush pilots and small independent airline companies between the wars, and miners were not their only passengers. By the end of this period missionaries, trappers, geologists, surveyors, Mounted Policemen, and eventually military personnel were dependent on them. Some of the early flights were remarkable for their length and the rugged terrain they traversed. As early as 1919 W.E. Catton flew on a mission from Winnipeg to Repulse Bay, NWT, to bring out a man with badly frozen hands for treatment, and in 1929 Leigh Brintnell, a pilot working for Western Canadian Airways, a company founded by the Richardson family of Winnipeg, flew from that city to Aklavik, dropping off Gilbert Labine at Great Bear Lake to look for pitchblende, then came back through Whitehorse and Edmonton, a trip of 15,000 kilometres. The airplane transformed the North. By 1935 more freight was being flown in Canada than in all the rest of the world combined, though of course much of it was in the northern provinces, particularly Ontario and Quebec, rather than in the territories.

The long-term consequences of mining development for the Northwest Territories were much the same as those of the Klondike gold rush for the Yukon. In the first place, it introduced modern technology to the region. Much of the exploration that led to the developments at Great Bear and Great Slave Lakes depended on air transport, which in turn led to the building of airfields, along with weather and radio facilities. A small petroleum field developed by the Imperial Oil Company at Norman Wells in 1920 proved particularly useful in this respect. River transport also changed, as the old steamboats that had carried passengers and small amounts of freight on the Mackenzie since the previous century gave way to large diesel tugs hauling barges: oil tanker barges, refrigerated barges, barges for other heavy cargo. A hydroelectric plant, the first in the NWT, came into operation on the Yellowknife River in 1941 to supply the town and the Consolidated Gold Mine. The town of Yellowknife, at first a haphazard collec-

Charles and Anne Lindbergh at Baker Lake, 1931, during one of their long-distance flights. HBC Archives, N9187.

tion of log cabins, began to develop as an administrative as well as a mining centre, foreshadowing its later role as territorial capital.

By 1939 there were 300 miners working at Yellowknife. Since many had brought their families north, it became necessary to think of schools, as well as a proper water supply and sewage system. Between 1931 and 1941 the white population of the Mackenzie district (the western half of the NWT) had increased from 782 (of whom 105 worked in missions) to over 2,400. In the same year the Indian population of the district was 4,000, and the mixed-blood or Métis population nearly 300. The Inuit population of the entire territory was 5,400. The non-Native population was thus not in a majority in the NWT, and it was highly concentrated in communities such as Yellowknife, pursuing occupations from which, as in the Yukon, the First Nations people were excluded, or in which they had no interest. Outside Yellowknife and Port Radium, life for the Native people continued much as it had since the first arrival of missionaries and traders a hundred years before.

Despite these developments, the arrangement by which the NWT was governed remained essentially unchanged for sixty years after the establishment of the territory in 1905. As all the Canadian provinces had been before Confederation, the NWT was governed by a legislative council. But this body was not responsible to the people of the region it governed, nor was it elected from their numbers—it did not even meet in the NWT. Instead, the Territorial Council, chaired by a commissioner, was made up of seven civil servants appointed by the federal government and met

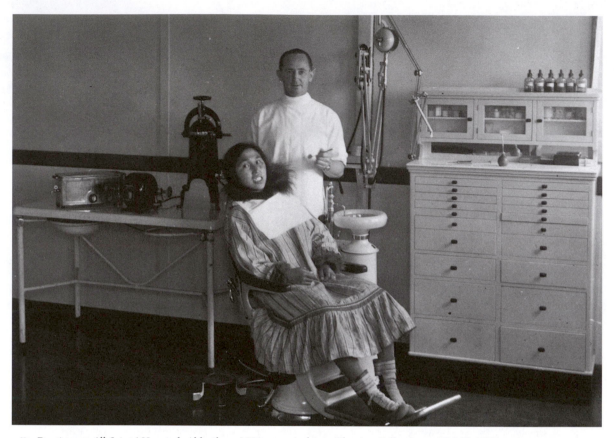

Dentistry at All Saints' Hospital, Aklavik, *c.* 1930. NWT Archives, Fleming Collection, N79-050:0076.

in Ottawa, originally only about once a year. The members of the council were those senior bureaucrats whose departments had some interest in the North; the first commissioner was Frederick Wood, comptroller (a sort of deputy minister) of the Mounted Police. Other members were drawn from the departments of Indian Affairs, the Interior, and, later, External Affairs. This convenient arrangement, resembling an informal super-committee of civil servants, worked quite well, though it was hopelessly undemocratic. It inherited all the legislative acts of the old North-West Territories, and had the power to pass new ordinances, which

it did at a leisurely pace—only twelve were passed during the 1920s. It was not until the advent of mining activities in the 1930s and, later, wartime defence projects that its business increased to any great extent, and not until long after the war's end that legislative activities actually took place in the NWT.

The Yukon retained its council in Dawson City even after the population of the territory shrank by 90 per cent, but it was a small and essentially powerless body. In 1918 membership in the Territorial Council was reduced to three. The federal subsidy to the Yukon was halved, forcing a purge of officials. Eventually the Yukon government was reduced in effect to a single person, George Jeckell. Jeckell had come to the Yukon during the gold rush to teach school. He became controller—that is, chief accountant—of the territory in 1913, and when the office of commissioner was abolished in 1918 as too grand and expensive for a community of 4,000, Jeckell became chief executive. Eventually, as the government shrank in what one commentator called 'a withering away of the state in a way that Marx never envisaged',[7] Jeckell acquired the offices of public works agent, income tax inspector, mayor of Dawson (ex officio), registrar of land title, and senior territorial executive. He ran the territory almost single-handedly until his retirement in 1948.

This was the state of the North on the eve of the Second World War: the Yukon in what seemed to be a permanent decline, its economy dependent on a small mining sector, and the NWT with a small but growing mining industry, but with most of its huge area and scattered population still largely unaffected by outsiders. The events of the next fifteen years, however, were to bring dramatic and permanent change to the region.

CHAPTER EIGHT

Invasion: War and the
Militarization of the North

By 1940, the first full year of the Second World War, the Canadian North had not changed very much since 1920, and not in any essential way since 1900. The Yukon was still a small mining community, with a small but viable fur trade, whose population had increased in twenty years from 4,000 to just over 5,000. The Northwest Territories, with a population approaching 9,000, had also changed very little. Except for the new mining centres it remained a land whose population was predominantly Indian and Inuit. The majority of the Inuit in the central and eastern Arctic lived off the land in the traditional manner, visiting the scattered trading posts to obtain whatever manufactured or processed goods they had incorporated into their way of life. For the most part they were left alone by the outside world; an annual visit from a government doctor, a regular patrol by the RCMP, a visit from a missionary, a trip to the trading post—this was the sum of their contact with mainstream society. Most Inuit had no formal education at all, except what itinerant missionaries might provide. Their medical care was rudimentary, and tuberculosis was already making serious inroads among them—a fact that the government ignored until after the war.

Before 1940 very few people thought of northern Canada in strategic terms, or considered the geopolitical role that the region might play. Vilhjalmur Stefansson was an important exception. In a series of widely read books published in the 1920s he advanced his vision of the north as a 'polar Mediterranean' and pioneered the idea of over-the-pole routes for aircraft and submarines. But as a northern visionary he was virtually alone: if Canadians thought of their North as the middle of anything, it was as the middle of nowhere.

Stefansson was not correct in all his prophecies and enthusiasms, but his geopolitical predictions for the North seemed completely justified in the years after 1940, albeit through events he had not foreseen. In 1941 the Canadian government began to construct a series of airfields from Edmonton to Fairbanks, mostly for defensive purposes, but also with the prospect of civil aviation in mind. The military and civilian airplanes of that day were incapable of very long uninterrupted flights, and needed landing fields for refuelling. As

A bulldozer crashing through the trees was sometimes the first notice northerners had that the Alaska Highway was being built. NA, 111-SC 139746.

well, weather stations and emergency landing fields were needed to support regular flights. As Stefansson and others had noted, the shortest route from the continental United States to the Far East lay over the Yukon and Alaska, and for this reason the airfields traced a path through northern British Columbia at Prince George, Fort St John, and Fort Nelson to Watson Lake and Whitehorse in the Yukon, and on to Fairbanks.

Not long after its construction began, the Northwest Staging Route was overshadowed by and absorbed into a much larger project.

The Japanese attack on Pearl Harbour, on 7 December 1941, which brought the United States into the war, also moved Alaska and the western half of the Canadian North from the periphery of national events to the front line of continental defence. Within a few weeks of the American declaration of war, a plan had been drawn up to build a highway that would link Alaska, through Canada, with the contiguous United States. The construction of this road, originally called the Alcan and later the Alaska Highway, and its ancillary facilities pushed the North once more into the national conscious-

Black troops of the US Army Engineers clearing the right of way at the southern end of the Alaska Highway, summer 1942. NA, 111-SC 139733.

ness, and radically altered the infrastructure, the economy, and the population balance both of the Yukon and of the Mackenzie district of the NWT. Northerners in both Canada and the United States had been campaigning for a highway throughout most of the 1930s, but the government had not been enthusiastic about spending the money required to build it. The war, however, swept away all considerations of economics and cost-effectiveness.

The purpose of the Alaska Highway was to provide a safe alternative to ocean communications between Alaska and the ports of the US Pacific northwest. Military planners feared that shipping would be vulnerable to Japanese submarines. Others, however, believed that the risk was overrated, and that the Japanese did not have the capacity to seriously disrupt shipping. Nevertheless, in the panicked atmosphere of early 1942 it was difficult to resist the pleas from Alaska for protection. Nor was the Canadian government, through whose territo-

Hauling supplies by pack train along the southern portion of the Alaska Highway, 1942. NA, 111-SC 144826.

ry most of the highway would run, disposed to resist the Americans' polite but insistent requests for co-operation in the project. Without much debate, Ottawa granted the Americans a free hand in the northwest to build the road wherever they liked, using whatever materials came to hand, so long as they agreed to pay for it and to turn it over the Canada at the end of the war.

A number of ancillary projects accompanied the highway, the most important of which was the Canol project. This involved the devel-opment of the small oil field at Norman Wells on the Mackenzie River, the construction of a pipeline from there to Whitehorse, nearly 1,000 kilometres away, and a refinery at Whitehorse to supply the Alaska Highway with petroleum products as far north as Fairbanks through another pipeline. The Northwest Staging Route was rapidly upgraded and completed, a tele-phone system was built (before the war the Yukon had relied on telegraph and radio tele-phone for outside communication), and all manner of other facilities were constructed.

US Army Engineers bridging a creek, 1942. These bridges were soon replaced by more permanent structures. NA, 111-SC 139940.

The Alaska Highway was one of the most remarkable feats of civil engineering ever carried out in North America, not because it was innovative in its conception or technique—it was just a dirt road, after all, and built to fairly low standards—but because it was so long, and was built so quickly under difficult conditions. From its beginning at Dawson Creek, BC, to its end at Fairbanks, Alaska, it stretched for more than 2,400 kilometres, and except at a few spots where rough roads and trails

already existed, it was constructed through a region about which almost everyone involved in its planning was totally ignorant. Despite great difficulties, the road was 'finished'—meaning that it was passable to heavy trucks so long as it was frozen—in only eight months, between March and November 1942.

This feat was made possible by a tremendous mobilization of men (along with a few women) and machinery. Nearly 40,000 people worked on the highway, the Canol project, and the various other projects that made up the continental defence effort in Alaska, the Yukon, and the NWT during the war. Such a huge influx—three times the entire population of both territories in 1941—was bound to leave its mark on the land. Further marks were made by the 11,000 pieces of heavy equipment brought north by the road- and pipeline-builders, from dump trucks to tractors and graders.

The initial construction of the Alaska Highway was undertaken by the US Army Corps of Engineers, whose tradition of civil and military engineering went back to 1779. Once the pioneer road was finished, it was widened, improved, and straightened by civilian contractors under the direction of the US Public Roads Administration, one of the New Deal agencies set up under the Roosevelt administration. Here the work was done by Canadians and Americans recruited for northern work by the contractors.

Begun in 1943 by the Corps of Engineers, and completed in 1945 by a civilian contractor, the Canol pipeline took longer to build than the highway. By the summer of 1943, even before construction started, it was fairly evident that Japan was not going to win the war, and that there was no real threat to the

Train leaving Skagway, Alaska, heading towards the White Pass and Canada with trucks and supplies for Alaska Highway construction. NA, 111-SC 150175.

supply of oil to Alaska by sea—hence no need for the project. Nevertheless it proceeded, propelled by the momentum of wartime enthusiasm and fuelled by cost-plus contracts. It was not taken very seriously at the time, and later commentators treated it as a kind of joke:

Today, to be sure, it is not easy to take Canol seriously. Its 4- and 6-inch pipeline, puny by our standards, was puny by the standards of the 1940s as well. Moreover, some of Canol's technology was the crudest to be found in the

modern repertoire: the wood stove, the pack horse, and the dog sled. . . it often proceeded like a situation comedy, as when the Mackenzie River mud swallowed whole vehicles, or a workman drove a truck through a mess hall after a lunch he did not like.[1]

Among the military and civilian workers who built the Canol morale was generally low. Many of the soldiers were Black; the American government, inspired by the crudely racist theories of the time, believed that Black people

Welding pipe along the Canol route. The finished pipe was laid on the bare ground. NAC, PA171533.

could not work well in cold weather, but they also wanted them far away from centres of population where racial clashes might occur, and racism won out over half-baked anthropological theories. When conscript soldiers from Mississippi and Alabama found themselves hauling freight at Fort Smith, NWT, or washing dishes in mess tents at Fort Norman, the result was resentment; only the presence of the military police prevented open defiance. The civilian workers, almost all of them white, were not any happier with their working con- ditions on the pipeline and road between Norman Wells and Whitehorse, which in its route over the Richardson Mountains traverses some of the remotest reaches of the North.

The technology used on the Canol project was primitive: the trees and brush were cut down or bulldozed, the soil scraped up to make a road, and the pipe laid directly on the ground. In addition the workmanship was shoddy and there was occasional sabotage, with the result that breaks and leaks were common. To bring nearly 1,000 kilometres of

A highway construction crew camped in an abandoned settlement in the southern Yukon, 1942. NAC, PA 130448.

steel pipe from the south to the Mackenzie Valley required the construction of roads, airfields, and bridges, as well as a barge system and other innovations. But cost overruns were enormous, and the price to the American government totalled $140 million (plus the unknown cost of the military input)—the same as for the entire Alaska Highway. The system operated intermittently for a year, and then on a reduced scale for another year, but in 1946 it was scrapped, the Whitehorse refinery was dismantled, and the pipe itself was taken apart and carted away. It has been aptly described by one historian as a 'junkyard monument to military stupidity'.[2]

The effect of these northwest defence projects on the indigenous population is a matter of some dispute. Native people who remember the building of the Alaska Highway cite it as a major turning-point in northern life. One common observation is that the men who built the highway treated the environment harshly, shooting every animal that came within the sights of their rifles, fishing the streams to

The pioneer road turned to quagmire in every rain. April 1942. NA, 111-SC 146243.

depletion, bringing disease, abusing women, and polluting both ground and water.

There is no doubt that the highway caused serious disruption in the life of the Native people of the southern Yukon and the Mackenzie Valley, who were not informed that it was to be built, let alone asked if they approved. In some cases the first intimation of change came when the bulldozers crashed through the bush into their communities. The fact that many of the early highway-builders were Black, the first Black people that the Native people had seen, only added to the confusion. And there were parts of the North that suffered serious epi-

demics. The worst affected was Teslin, in the southern Yukon, which experienced epidemics of measles, pneumonia, and influenza in the winter of 1942–43, not because the residents had never been exposed to outsiders, but because the other white people they had been exposed to had spent weeks getting into the country, and were generally not infectious. Many of the newcomers had flown in from Edmonton in a matter of hours. The result was that in 1942 and 1943 there were more deaths than births among the Indians of the southern Yukon, and the populations both of children and of elders—the ones who transmitted the

The US Army built a tent city at Whitehorse in the spring of 1942. NA, 111-SC 150168.

culture from generation to generation—were seriously depleted.

There is also truth in the other charges. The military and civilian workers were permitted to hunt for recreation and to provide fresh meat as a supplement to the tedious and unappetizing military rations, and some did vigorously pursue every animal that crossed their path; however, most of the men lacked the skills necessary to hunt effectively in the bush, or even to keep from getting lost, and the depletion of game was confined to a fairly narrow corridor. Some rivers were temporarily fished out, and countless trees were cut down

for bridge and culvert building, and to heat the camps and buildings (the air force operations at Whitehorse burned 10,000 cords, a stupendous amount, in the winter of 1942–43), although they would eventually grow again. The most lasting damage was caused by the careless construction techniques that ruined streams and the fuel spills that lingered for years. In 1976 Joe Jacquot, a famous Yukon guide, described the results of one wartime fuel spill:

When the line was cut the fuel ran into pockets and disappeared. Some went into peat

Clearing stumps in the southern Yukon, summer 1942. NA, 111-SC 148518.

bogs that acted as a large sponge. When the spring breakup came and the spring run-off was in effect, fuel flowed not only into the lakes but into the streams. The migratory birds heading north at this time became unknowing victims. The muskrat and beaver died. Some of those lakes still don't have rat houses on them. Up until about 4 years ago the people couldn't eat the fish in Swede Johnson Creek because they tasted of fuel oil.[3]

Today such incidents would be seen as scandalous, but in the 1940s the environmental impact studies that are routine today were undreamed of, and the exigencies of the war silenced any opposition that might otherwise have been expressed. There was very little information available on such topics as construction in permafrost zones, and the Canol pipeline, for instance, was built in a manner that guaranteed environmental damage. Stripping off the shrubs and turf and laying the pipe directly on the ground ensured that the permafrost would thaw, the ground would subside, and the pipeline would break, pouring out oil. The projects took place in an atmosphere of environmental unconsciousness, and the builders neither knew nor cared about

Trucks that broke down were often abandoned and stripped for spare parts. US Engineers photo.

the long-term results of their activities. The point was to get the job done.

The only environmental impact that the military and civilian builders paid much attention to was the danger of forest fire, probably because that was the one actual threat to the personnel in the region. Fires were touched off by careless smokers, by poor storage of petroleum products, by the huge piles of brush left by the bulldozers, and by the smoky fires built to keep mosquitoes at bay. One fire of this last type, begun in the summer of 1943 near Fort Smith, NWT, burned through the moss and muskeg for months, and at one point destroyed

the Roman Catholic mission in the community.

On the other hand, the wartime assault on the environment also resulted in a new awareness, in official quarters, of the importance of conservation. In the southwest Yukon, hunting was putting considerable pressure on the populations of large mammals such as moose and Dall sheep. Accordingly, in 1942 the federal government set up the Kluane game preserve, a preliminary step in the establishment of Kluane National Park, now a UNESCO World Heritage Site. That the First Nations people were also excluded from hunting in this preserve, an area that had supplied them with

There were several 'suicide hills' on the highway. This photo was made into a postcard; the caption reads 'View Along the New Alcan Highway through Canada's Wilderness Built by a Welcome Army of U.S. Soldiers'. Author's collection.

food for countless generations, was a side effect that seemed to concern no one else. As well as providing impetus for this important park, the Alaska Highway made it easier for scientists to travel north, and even before the end of the war, biologists from the University of British Columbia, the Royal Ontario Museum, Harvard University, and the National Museum of Canada had visited the region to conduct surveys and research.

Another effect of the defence projects was an unprecedented diminution of Canada's control over its own North. Even in the days of the Klondike gold rush, when the population of the Yukon was overwhelmingly non-Canadian,

the federal government had been quick to send the Mounted Police to the region to show the flag and prove Canadian sovereignty over it. With respect to the Alaska Highway and Canol projects, however, Ottawa simply abandoned any semblance of control. During the initial period of construction, a lone government representative, C.K. LeCapelain, acted as liaison officer between the entire American presence and the Canadian government. It was not until Malcolm Macdonald, the British High Commissioner, made a tour of the northwest and reported to Ottawa that the Americans were operating as if they owned the country that the government appointed a special com-

Opening ceremonies were held in sub-zero weather at Soldier's Summit, west of Whitehorse, on 20 November 1942.
NA, 111-SC 164887.

missioner, Major-General W.W. Foster, to represent Canadian interests in the region. But one or two men could have little effect in such a vast region where the issues involved were so far-reaching.

In fact, Ottawa went to considerable lengths to facilitate American operations in the North. The federal government passed a law making American troops working in Canada answerable only to US military courts, and this immunity to Canadian law was extended to American civilians working on the defence projects. Policing both the Highway and Canol projects was the responsibility of American Military Police, who dealt forcefully with sol-

diers and civilians alike—Canadians as well as Americans. In the isolated regions this did not affect many people, but where the Alaska Highway went through centres of population such as Dawson Creek, BC, and Whitehorse their presence was an irritant. They controlled the line-ups at the liquor store, patrolled the streets, demanded identification from drivers, politely or otherwise, and tried unsuccessfully to stem the importation of bootleg liquor into the North. A minor refrain in the region throughout this period was the question 'Whose country is this, anyway?' But the RCMP, whose numbers in the North were small (only 20 in the Yukon in 1940), welcomed the assis-

The Alaska Highway was built at tremendous speed and without much concern for engineering principles. Much of it had to be rebuilt when bridges and rights of way washed out in the spring of 1943. This bridge was a casualty; its replacement can be seen in the background. Author's collection.

tance, and co-operated in a friendly fashion with the American MPs.

Some of the most dramatic effects of the wartime defence projects were experienced by the communities involved. The more southerly cities that acted as bases for the projects welcomed the influx of American personnel and the cash it injected into local economies; in Edmonton, the general administrative headquarters for the projects, the Americans bought 400,000 board feet of lumber and $30,000 worth of tools in the spring of 1942 alone. Some American headquarters personnel also

made their presence felt in more personal ways: between 1942 and 1945, approximately fifty of them married Canadian women.

But Edmonton was a large city, capable of accommodating the Americans without too much strain. Much more striking was the impact on small, remote communities, particularly in the Yukon. The effects on places such as Fort Smith and Norman Wells, in the NWT, were short-lived, since the Canol project did not survive the war. The men actually building the highway, pipeline, and other facilities lived on-site, in tent communities that were moved

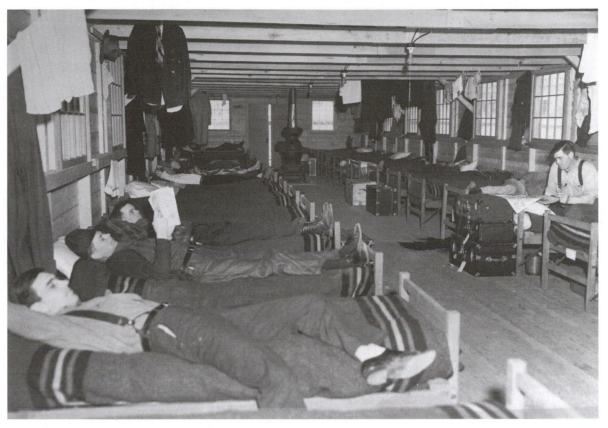

A bunkhouse for civilian construction workers, somewhere along the highway. They had few leisure activities, and most preferred long hours of paid overtime to doing nothing. US Engineers photo.

along the road as construction proceeded. But the projects also required thousands of support staff: men and women who actually lived in the local communities. These towns were small by any standard. The summer population of Whitehorse in the census of 1941 was 754, and a good deal less than that in the winter, yet by April 1943 it was home to more than 10,000 people, four-fifths of them Americans.

Some of these newcomers lived in tents, some in barracks and Quonset huts, which were built by the score, and some in a variety of ramshackle dwellings thrown up around the town. The military provided housing of a kind

for all its people, but civilians arriving to work on the projects had to find their own accommodation. Some were reduced to squatting in shacks made of packing crates on the bank of the Yukon River. A new movie theatre was built, along with a new water supply and sewer system. And in response to the civilian housing crisis, a local entrepreneur named Martin Berrigan built several 'log skyscrapers'—log houses three stories high—one of which still survives as a tourist attraction. By the end of the war the US had put over $9 million, and Canada $2 million, into local construction projects.

Trucks had to travel the first crude road in convoys. Much of it was subsequently rebuilt, during and after the war. NA, 111-SC 139950.

The regional transportation system was also severely affected by the war. The White Pass and Yukon Railway, with its subsidiary steamboat company, which controlled traffic on the Yukon River, had operated at a profit since the line's opening in 1900, exercising a monopoly over passenger and freight traffic into the Canadian far northwest. The plan for the Alaska Highway was to begin construction from the north at Fairbanks, from the south at Dawson Creek, and from the middle at Whitehorse going both north and south. This necessitated moving huge amounts of supplies and equipment of all kinds over the railway from tidewater at Skagway to Whitehorse. The WP&YR's small-scale and rather leisurely operations were swamped by the demands of the Americans, and in October 1942 the Northwest Service Command took over the railway, operating it for the rest of the war. Civilian passenger traffic was reduced to two trains a week, freight trains ran almost continuously, and at the end of the war, when the army handed the line back to its owners, its track and rolling stock were so worn out that considerable capital investment was required to make it operable again.

For Whitehorse, as can be imagined, a

Civilian contractors' mess hall. The food was plentiful but monotonous. The civilian workers were older than the average soldier, often too old to be drafted. US Engineers photo.

twelvefold population increase in the space of a year affected every facet of life. The Bank of Commerce, the only bank in town, where Robert Service had once worked, had so much new business that its staff was increased from three to twelve. Monthly liquor sales in town increased from $7,000 in April 1942 to $87,000 in December, and by March 1944 the territorial liquor account showed a surplus of $400,000, most of it coming from Whitehorse. The Americans' enthusiasm for their national pastime led to the construction of baseball diamonds all over town; at the end of the war it was said that Whitehorse had more baseball

facilities per capita than any community in North America.

A change of a different kind occurred in Dawson City, the old gold-rush town and territorial capital. In 1941 it still housed the administration of the Yukon, was the centre of the gold mining industry, and had a population slightly larger than that of its southern rival. One of the routes proposed for the Alaska Highway would have gone north to Dawson City and then west to Fairbanks. But the route chosen, through Whitehorse, doomed the old town to a declining future. Because Whitehorse was linked to the southern road network through the Alaska Highway, it survived the war as a transportation centre. In 1946 the population of Whitehorse was still 3,680, while Dawson City's was only 688. The more northerly community was not linked to the outside by road until ten years after the end of the war. By 1950 it was clear that the territorial capital would have to be moved to Whitehorse; this was done in 1953, over the strenuous objections of Dawson City's residents. The old town was eventually saved not by the mining industry, which was also near its end, but by the federal government, which in the 1960s began to restore it as a tourist attraction.

The wartime defence effort in the Canadian North was not confined to the Alaska Highway and Canol projects, though these were its largest components. The American military machine touched and transformed other parts of the country as well. The air route from North America to Europe required new landing fields and weather stations. Frobisher Bay (now Iqaluit) was founded during the war as a weather station on the site of a traditional Inuit fishing camp. It survived the war to become the administrative centre of the eastern Arctic, changed its name from English to Inuktitut, and will become the capital of the new territory of Nunavut in 1999. The airport at Gander, Newfoundland (not part of Canada until 1949), though begun before the war, was greatly expanded, and new facilities were built at Goose Bay, Labrador, and elsewhere.

At the end of the war the Alaska Highway, the Canol project, and all the ancillary facilities were turned over to the Canadian government. They brought permanent change to the territories. In addition to 2,400 kilometres of more-or-less finished road, a pipeline, a refin-

ery, and a telephone system running from Edmonton to the Yukon–Alaska boundary, the Americans had constructed seven weather forecasting and seventeen weather reporting stations. They had put $16 million into upgrading the port of Prince Rupert (another transportation gateway to the northern interior) and built a 250-bed hospital in Edmonton. Along the transportation route from Edmonton to the oilfield at Fort Norman, they had built a wharf, rail facilities, storage, housing, and a refrigeration unit at Waterways in northern Alberta; a wharf, warehouse, and freight complex at Fitzgerald; freight and gasoline storage facilities at Fort Smith (where they also improved the road); freight transfer facilities at Resdelta; a freight and docking complex at Fort Providence; an airfield at Fort Simpson; and freight facilities at Wrigley. They had established radio broadcasting stations at Whitehorse, Fort Nelson, Watson Lake, Fort Simpson, and Norman Wells, as well as hundreds of other facilities, large and small, throughout the western part of the Canadian North.

Though the departure of the Americans from northern Canada, largely completed by the end of 1946, was amicable on both sides—the Americans were glad to leave, and the Canadians were glad to see them go—the process of disengagement from such a massive operation inevitably caused some friction. The closing of the Canol project was a severe disappointment to northern residents, who had viewed it as a cornerstone of post-war prosperity, relieving them from dependence on expensive imported fuel. But the project had been an embarrassment to the American government. Late in the war, a US Senate commit-

The tent city at Whitehorse was replaced by more permanent structures, many of which were put to civilian use after the war. Author's collection.

tee headed by Senator Harry Truman had investigated waste and boondoggles in military spending, and the Canol project had been one of its principal exhibits. Neither Washington nor Ottawa was interested in keeping the line functioning, and in 1947 it was cut up and taken back to the United States.

The issue that caused the most bad feeling in northern Canada at the end of the war, however, and the one that lingered longest in local memory, concerned the disposition of surplus goods and equipment used in the projects. Much of the heavy equipment—trucks, jeeps, and the like—was taken back to the US.

But there were also vast amounts of smaller goods and equipment—everything from canned goods to bedsheets to cast-iron stoves—stored in warehouses all over the North. Local residents hoped and expected that these supplies would be abandoned for them to take, or at least sold to them for a few cents on the dollar. But this did not happen, partly because the Canadian government feared the effect such a policy would have on local retailers, and partly because the Americans did not want hordes of Canadians scrounging and pilfering their equipment. The official policy was that everything worth saving

A pioneer bridge and temporary work camp on an unnamed river along the highway, summer 1942. NA, 111-SC 139947.

had to be taken south, and anything left had to be destroyed. The actual policy was to destroy a great deal of useful material, to the dismay of northerners. One Whitehorse resident reported seeing 'a barracks between two and three city blocks long, packed with winter clothes, parkas, pure wool blankets, comforters, chairs, office desks, and almost everything else you could imagine. They stacked them up, poured gasoline over them, set them on fire. Guards stood over them so nobody could get anything.'[4] Fifty years after these events, it is difficult to separate fact from fiction. The Americans indignantly denied that there had been any such bonfire, claiming that only goods of no value were destroyed. But pho-

tographs of dumps along the highway clearly show unused engine parts, an axle in its original packing, unused piles of sheet steel—all presumably useful to some local resident. Whatever the truth—and certainly value is in the eye of the beholder; what was surplus to the Americans could be treasure to northerners—the episode led to an enduring local legend that the Americans, in a fit of dog-in-the-manger selfishness, had decided to destroy what they could not take home. Happily, many enterprising residents took matters into their own hands and 'liberated' quantities of useful goods for themselves.

When Canada took over the Alaska Highway, in the spring of 1946, it was in doubtful shape. Much of the original pioneer road had been upgraded by the US Public Roads Administration, but much work needed to be done. The original bridges and culverts had been rugged log affairs, and most needed to be replaced. Most people, Canadian and American, assumed that it would be opened to civilian traffic, but because it was so rough, and there were no facilities along the route (in 1947 there was only one civilian garage between Fort St John and Whitehorse), this was not allowed without a special permit until 1948.

From the northern point of view, the wartime projects were a mixed success. They had brought about an astonishing transformation of the regions where they were built. But there were some disappointments. Regional boosters had hoped that many of the military and civilian workers who had served in the area would return after the war to settle there, but few did. Yet the road was in place, and gradually tourist camps, roadhouses, and service stations were opened beside it. For twenty years after the war the Alaska Highway remained mostly unpaved, and its gravel surface caused such wear and tear on automobiles that it kept many garages in business. Later, of course, when that surface was improved, many of these were forced to close. Northerners hoped for a vastly increased tourist trade once it was possible for southerners to visit the Yukon by car. The trade did increase, although by far the largest number of people using the Alaska Highway over the years have not been tourists as such, but Americans driving to and from what eventually became the 49th state.

The Canol project was a greater disappointment. After the pipeline was removed, the road that serviced it was allowed to decay, and within a year or two after the war it was no longer possible to drive from Whitehorse to Norman Wells. Eventually the NWT section of the road was completely abandoned, though part of the Yukon section was incorporated into that territory's highway system.

The western part of the Canadian North, however, never returned to its pre-war condition. The population of Whitehorse fell by two-thirds immediately after the war, from more than 10,000 in 1943 to about 3,600 in 1946. But this still was a huge increase over the 1941 population of 750, and in the years after the war the town started to grow again as the government presence in the North began to increase. The network of transportation, communications, and other facilities left over from the war was equally huge, and the local population took advantage of it. Most of the buildings constructed to serve the road and pipeline builders were sold to local interests at bargain prices, and for decades after the war these 'temporary buildings' were a notable feature of the northern urban landscape, as they were of most Canadian cities until the 1970s. The Whitehorse Indian Baptist school, for instance, was housed for years in war-surplus buildings, and the American military hospital in Edmonton was taken over by the federal government and used for Native patients. Over wide areas of the Canadian North, more in the west but in the east as well, the war left a legacy that still endures.

CHAPTER NINE

The New North:
The Age of Development

*I*n the quarter-century after the end of the Second World War, the Canadian North underwent transformations that made the changes of the previous century pale by comparison. Many forces contributed: increased resource development, urbanization, a more far-flung militarization, and, at the end of the period, a political awakening among the northern First Nations. However, the force that had the most dramatic effect on Native people in this period was the advent of the Canadian social welfare state.

Before 1940, the federal government had based its policy with respect to the Indians and, even more, the Inuit of the Yukon and Northwest Territories on the position that the less their indigenous way of life was interfered with, the better. According to the official view, it was impossible—and undesirable in any case—to integrate them into the wider Canadian society; therefore they should be left alone to pursue their traditional occupations on the land. What education was necessary could be provided by church mission schools, while health care could be handled by small subsidies to doctors (in the Yukon), or by peri-

odic visits from medical missionaries or itinerant government doctors (in the NWT). This policy was well suited to a government that, strapped for cash during the Depression, was unwilling to take on new obligations. It was largely for this reason that Treaty 11, signed with the Dene of the Mackenzie Valley in 1921, had never been fully implemented, and that no treaty was proposed to the First Nations of the Yukon or to the Inuit.

All this changed after 1945. A basic premise of the post-war world was that life should be better for everyone; in the words of the unfulfilled promise made in Britain after the First World War, there would be 'homes fit for heroes'. This philosophy was reflected in the administrations of W.L. Mackenzie King, prime minister from 1935 to 1948 (and from 1921 to 1926, and 1926 to 1930), and his successor, Louis St Laurent (1948–57), who combined a willingness to spend money on programs of social improvement with a desire to win favour by giving the public what it seemed to want. Thus in the post-war years a cornucopia of benefits was showered on the public, including First Nations: modest ones at first, but then more generous.

As conservative economists never tire of reminding us, government cornucopias often come with strings attached, and have consequences that their benevolent proponents do not necessarily intend. The best example of this principle in action in the North is the Mothers' Allowance. This plan, popularly called the 'baby bonus', was introduced in 1944 as a means of putting some cash in the pockets of mothers of young children. Mothers were given $5 per month for each child under the age of 16—not a large sum by today's standards, but for large families in cash-poor regions it could make a significant difference. Indeed, since families of twenty children were not unknown in Quebec, it was said in Ontario that the scheme was designed simply to buy French-Canadian votes.

The Mothers' Allowance was provided to women in all regions and of all races. But whereas in the provinces it was always paid by cheque, to Indians along with everyone else, in the two territories it was paid to the Native people, though not non-Natives, in kind. The philosophy behind this policy was pure paternalism: in the government's view the northern First Nations people were not sufficiently educated or mature to make the proper choices in spending the money. Thus it was given to them in the form of groceries and supplies at stores and trading posts. There was a list of approved goods: evaporated milk was on the list, because it could be fed to children, while condensed milk, which was sweetened, was not, because it could be used to make candy. Similarly, rolled oats for porridge were approved, while prepared, sweetened breakfast cereals were not. One might see a kind of logic in this policy for the Inuit in the central Arctic, whose

Mother and child. The can of powdered Klim ('milk' spelled backwards) was perhaps the fruit of the new Mothers' Allowance. NAC, PA147029.

contact with the outside world was quite recent, but plainly in the case of the Indians of the Yukon, who had been in close, though intermittent, contact with the mainstream culture for fifty years, it was insulting.

This was not the only element of social engineering in the Mothers' Allowance, however. In order for the mother to receive it, the child, if of school age, had to be attending school. Before the war, formal classroom education for the Native children of northern Canada ranged from none at all for most Inuit and many Indians to a rudimentary elementary education for some Indian children in residential schools run by churches—four or five of them across the entire territorial North—or in day schools operated for short periods by mis-

Yellowknife in 1947 was a vigorous, raffish place, the industrial capital of the Northwest Territories. NAC, PA116541.

sionaries. Given the importance of the Mothers' Allowance to families with low cash incomes, a group that included most northern Native people, this provision served as a powerful incentive for parents to send their children to school.

At the same time, northern schools were becoming secularized: increasing numbers of their teachers were lay people rather than clergy, with salaries paid by the department of Indian Affairs rather than the churches. The growth of the public schools, now racially integrated, hastened the process of secularization. The Northwest Territories proved a particular problem, since its Native population was scattered among many small communities, and in the 1950s a good number of Inuit still lived entirely on the land. In response to this problem the government constructed large schools and residences in the major communities—Fort McPherson, Inuvik, Fort Simpson, Fort Smith, and Frobisher Bay (Iqaluit)—and small schools in 57 other communities. By 1958 only half of all school-age Native children were regularly attending school. Ten years later the figure was 90 per cent; the school population ranged from over a thousand at Inuvik to fewer than twenty at places like Padloping Island and Fort Liard.

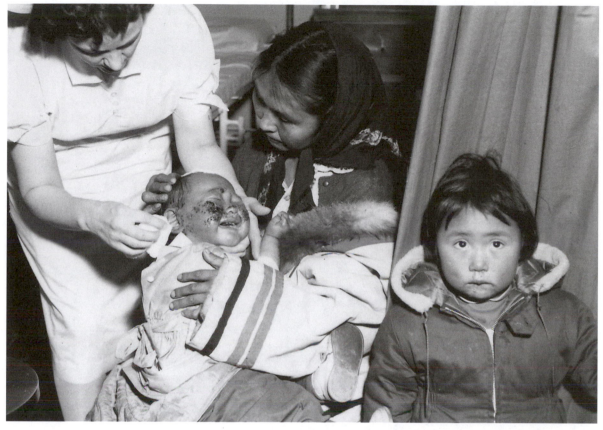

An Inuit child being treated for impetigo. Improved medical care after the Second World War led to dramatic improvements in health among Inuit. NAC, PA141908.

But school buildings alone did not guarantee education, and Native pupils experienced many difficulties. One problem was that the authorities could not decide on a goal for education. At first it was 'to assist acculturation . . . and to prepare Indian youth for economic competence and social stability'. For this reason, the schools initially adopted southern school curricula wholesale, sometimes with additional courses in subjects of local interest, such as trapping. The authorities felt that competence in English or French was vitally important, and because fewer than half the children beginning school spoke anything but their Native languages, great emphasis was put on this. Children were forbidden to speak their ancestral languages and infractions were punished, sometimes physically. Beatings for 'talking Indian' were, along with incidents of sexual abuse and the prolonged absences from home caused by the vast distances between many of the schools and their home communities, among the most bitter experiences that former students remember today from their schooling. Roman Catholic Indians from the northern Yukon, for example, could not attend

Some of Dawson City's buildings were close to collapse by 1960. This one was not restored, but was left as a picturesque ruin for tourists to photograph. Yukon Government photo.

the large boarding school at Carcross, because it was traditionally Anglican. Instead they went to the nearest Catholic school, at Lower Post on the Yukon–British Columbia border, many hundreds of kilometres away. The costs and inconvenience of transportation were such that some students did not return home even in the summer, but spent six years or more at the school. When they returned home they were strangers to their families and communities, lacking both the bush and the family skills to make them fully functioning members of their people. The result for many was 'mission

school syndrome', an alienation from both Native and non-Native worlds that often led to alcoholism, violence, and despair.

There were other, lesser difficulties: a large turnover among teachers, many teachers who knew nothing about Native culture, the lack of employment opportunities at the end of schooling, which led people to question its value. But if the First Nations of the North were unclear on the purpose of their children's education, the federal government had no doubt. It was all part of the post-war social welfare state, in which class and racial distinctions were to

This gold-rush era church moulders silently beside Lake Bennett. Author's collection.

be eliminated and all Canadian citizens were to receive equal benefits. It was in this spirit that the Old Age Pension became universal in the 1950s, benefiting the rich as well as the poor. All citizens were to be treated in the same manner; thus discriminatory regulations were repealed, and Native people were permitted to vote, drink alcohol, and resume once-banned customs such as the potlatch. These changes culminated in the Trudeau government's White Paper on Indian Policy of 1969, which advocated the abolition of the reserves and the assimilation of Native people into the Canadian mosaic as just another ethnic group.

In the 1950s the indigenous people of the North began to receive even more attention from the federal government, particularly because in some ways they were the most disadvantaged people in Canada, a fact that was brought spectacularly to the attention of the public through two books by Farley Mowat, reputedly Canada's most widely read author: *People of the Deer* (1952) and *The Desperate People* (1959). In these books he depicted the misery of the Inuit of Ennadai, in the Barrens of the Keewatin district north of Manitoba, who in the late 1940s had been reduced to such destitution that many starved to death.

By the 1960s snowmobiles were replacing dog teams. Here Methuselah Kunuk hunts near Iqaluit, 1987. NWT Government photo.

The books created a scandal and impelled the government to focus more attention on social programs in the North.

The new emphasis on health care was long overdue. When in 1947 the government began to test northerners for tuberculosis, it was found to be rampant. A new TB wing at the Whitehorse hospital handled many cases, but others had to be sent to Edmonton and even farther south. In the early 1950s the sanatorium at Hamilton, Ontario, whose business was falling off because of declining TB rates among whites, found new patients in the dozens of Inuit who were sent there for recovery. Some died, but more were cured and returned home, sometimes after years of absence. At the same time, as the indigenous people moved into communities across the North, they gained access to care in clinics and hospitals, and their health improved. Soon their numbers began to increase dramatically.

Along with education and health care came a host of other government programs for the North: housing, adult education, cultural programs, wildlife conservation, economic development, and many others, including a wide variety of programs aimed at social problems such as domestic violence, alcoholism,

The ss *Keno*, one of the last river steamers, attracts tourists in Dawson City. Yukon Government photo.

and, eventually, drug abuse. One result of this new interventionist policy was that the bureaucracy charged with the administration of the North, once minuscule, became enormous. In 1957, at the end of the St Laurent administration, there were over 3,200 full-time and 2,000 seasonal federal employees living in the North and serving a population of just 31,500. In less than forty years government had gone from being a negligible presence in the Northwest Territories to being the region's largest employer.

Of all the social engineering that took place in this period involving northern First Nations, the episode that has been the most controversial in the present day took place more than four decades ago. This was the relocation of a number of Inuit from Pond Inlet on Baffin Island and the Quebec shore of Hudson Bay to new communities at Resolute, on the south coast of Cornwallis Island, and Craig Harbour, on the south coast of Ellesmere Island. At the centre of the controversy is whether this move, which involved the transfer of families many hundreds of kilometres north to regions they knew nothing of, was voluntary or coerced. The government's motivation has also come under question. At the time, the move was portrayed as a humanitarian gesture, a transfer of people on the verge of starvation to a region where the hunting was much better. It turned out that, contrary to what some southerners might have thought, the Inuit are not a uniform people, interchangeable as individuals, happy to live wherever there is ice. The people from northern Quebec, well south of the Arctic circle, barely survived in a new home where it was dark for weeks on end in the winter, and where hunting was not as good as had been promised. It is now alleged, moreover, that at least part of the impetus came from the government's desire, at the height of the Cold War, to strengthen Canadian sovereignty in the high Arctic by increasing its population, for even the few families relocated to Craig Harbour represented a huge increase over the previous indigenous population of Ellesmere Island, which was zero.

Some of those who made the move now claim that they were coerced into it by government officials and the RCMP, an assertion that may or may not be true. It is true that few Inuit of that day would have known that they had civil rights—let alone what they were or how to assert them—and that most were anxious to comply with the wishes of the authorities. What critics of the episode forget, however, is the power in government affairs of what might be called the 'embarrassment factor'. The relocation episode took place in 1953, a year after the publication of Mowat's *People of the Deer*, which had excoriated the federal government for neglecting its Inuit wards in the Barrenlands. The suggestion that Canada, a rich industrialized country, was letting its citizens starve in the midst of plenty was seriously embarrassing to Ottawa, and when it was suggested that other Inuit groups were threatened

with the same fate, the government was not slow to act. Having a population of Canadians resident on Ellesmere Island was a bonus. The authors of *Tammarniit* ('Mistakes'), a recent book on the episode, conclude: 'What started out as a concern for the deteriorating welfare conditions of Inuit in Arctic Quebec was to become entangled in the minds of some officials . . . with concerns about sovereignty and the enforcement of Canadian law in the Arctic Archipelago, both of which were fuelled by cold war fears, Soviet atomic capability, and American military paranoia.'[1] Such paternalist tinkering with the lives of Native people was not uncommon forty years ago; that such an episode would presumably be unthinkable today shows how much times have changed.

Among the other changes of this period was a boom in resource development. The post-war world was hungry for raw materials and minerals of all kinds, and these the Canadian North was ready and willing to provide. Although mineral exploration and development continued throughout this period, it reached its height in the 1960s, at a time when northern resource development had become a national catchword. The government of John Diefenbaker (1957–63) talked much of a 'northern vision' and 'roads to resources', the idea being that the North was a treasurehouse of wealth that could be used both to develop the region and to bring prosperity to the country as a whole. Diefenbaker saw the North as a counterweight to the tremendous force exerted on Canada by the United States, a country he disliked and mistrusted. In his view the vast, undeveloped North held the key to Canada's future. Like John A. Macdonald, the country's first prime minister, of whom he believed

Whitehorse is a modern city with more amenities than most places its size. The Yukon government complex is in the centre of the picture. The park in the foreground was once 'Whiskey Flats', the home of some of the Territory's 'colourful five percent', until they were displaced in a campaign of civic beautification. Yukon Government photo.

himself to be the political reincarnation, he called for a 'National Policy', this time for the North. Some progress was made under Alvin Hamilton, minister of Northern Affairs from 1957 to 1960, as the northern communications system was improved, exploration for oil and minerals was encouraged, and social programs were extended to northern Native people. There were some parallels between the old National Policy, which had led to the settlement of the Prairies and the construction of the Canadian Pacific Railway, and the new northern one, perhaps the most notable being

the support provided for a railway to be built from northern Alberta to the new mines at Pine Point, NWT. Like Macdonald's CPR, this railway was built to open new economic opportunities and to link various regions of the country, particularly economically. The Roads to Resources program led to the beginning of the first all-weather highway linking the Arctic with the southern road system. This was the Dempster Highway, planned to link Dawson City with Fort McPherson and Inuvik. Begun during Diefenbaker's term in office, it was not finished until 1978. The Mackenzie

Preparing sealskins, Lake Harbour, 1967. Old skills have not been lost in the North, though some of them now have to be taught as courses in school. NWT Archives, Smith Collection, N91-028:0067.

Highway was built in the same period, linking Edmonton with Yellowknife and Fort Smith and continuing north to the end of the road at Wrigley. Unlike Macdonald, however, Diefenbaker had neither the persistence nor the political skill to make his vision a reality, and when his political troubles began to overwhelm him, he lost interest in it.

The year 1964 saw the passing of one northern industry and the beginning of a new one. In that year the Yukon Consolidated Gold Company went out of business, and the last dredge working the old Klondike creeks ceased operations. After seventy years it was the end of large corporate gold mining in the Yukon, though individual miners continued to work the creeks on a small scale. In the same year, however, the extraction of lead and zinc began on a large scale at Pine Point, on the south shore of Great Slave Lake. Cominco began operations the next year, and in two years the value of minerals produced in the NWT rose from $18.6 million to $115 million. In the Yukon a new lead-zinc mining operaton was developed at Faro, boosting mineral production in the Yukon from a value of $14.7 million in 1967 to nearly $230 million in 1975. Other mines and mining communities were estab-

John Snowshoe, Renewable Resource Officer with the NWT government, talking to trapper Peter Vittrekwa, near Fort McPherson, 1988. NWT Government photo.

lished at Clinton Creek, west of Dawson City, where asbestos was mined beginning in 1967, and near Whitehorse, where a large open-pit copper mine went into production in the same year. The dreams of Vilhjalmur Stefansson and other Arctic boosters were realized when in 1970 the discovery was announced of huge oil and natural gas deposits in the Beaufort Sea, off the northern coast of the Yukon and the Mackenzie Delta near Tuktoyaktuk.

All this new economic activity, combined with a greatly increased government presence and a significant decrease in Native mortality rates brought about by improved nutrition and health care, led to a rapid rise in the population of the North. Between 1961 and 1966 the population of the Northwest Territories rose from 23,000 to nearly 29,000, and in another five years to nearly 35,000. Ten years later, in 1981, it had reached 46,000, and in the mid-1990s it stood at approximately 60,000. The Yukon's population rose rapidly as well, particularly in the latter half of the 1960s, when it grew by nearly a third, from 14,000 to 18,000; by 1981 it was 23,000; and by 1995 it had reached 30,000.

It was during this era that the people of the North, and particularly the NWT, became urbanized. In 1940 most of the First Nations, especially the Inuit, still lived on the land, visiting settled communities only periodically. Within a quarter-century of the end of the war there was virtually no one in the Canadian North who lived in this fashion. The First Nations kept their close affinity with the land, using it, as they still do, as a source of food, of recreation, and of spiritual renewal. But by the end of the 1960s virtually the entire population lived in communities, drawn there by the services they offered: education, housing, social assistance, and the rest. When in the mid-1960s a National Film Board crew, aided by an anthropologist, made the Netsilik Eskimo Series, twenty hour-long films about the traditional life of an Inuit family at Igloolik, they had to settle for a family that had recently moved off the land. They went back to living the traditional way for a year while the films were made. In the end, the series was authentic enough, but even at its début it was a museum piece.

With the end of the Second World War the Cold War began, spreading a new militarism around the world in which the Canadian North played an important part. In contrast to the Alaska Highway, which in retrospect could be seen as a public-works project with debatable military value, the post-war military projects carried out in northern Canada were indisputably strategic, many with no civilian value at all. The reason for this new military presence in the region was, of course, the fact that after 1945 the United States and its allies perceived a new enemy in the Soviet Union, and the physical frontier between the USSR and what was generally called the 'free world' was the Canadian North. For this reason, between 1945 and 1960 vast military expenditures were made in the North, particularly in the high Arctic and along the Arctic coast.

The new militarization of the North began with 'Exercise Musk-Ox', a military training exercise conducted by the Canadian Army in the early months of 1946. It involved sending a force of forty men from Churchill, Manitoba, to Baker Lake and the Arctic coast at Coppermine, then from Fort Norman to Fort Nelson on the Alaska Highway, a distance of 5,000 kilometres. The purpose was to demonstrate that the Canadian Armed Forces could operate successfully in a northern winter.

More substantial projects began in 1947 with the construction by Canada and the United States of a series of weather stations in the high Arctic, at Resolute, Mould Bay, Isachsen, Eureka, and Alert; the latter station, built in 1950, lay at the northern tip of Ellesmere Island, by a considerable distance the most northerly inhabited place in the Western hemisphere. These were followed by a much more massive project designed to protect North America from what was perceived to be the main threat of the Cold War: attack by long-range airplanes carrying nuclear bombs. This was the Distant Early Warning (DEW) line, a series of radar stations stretching from Alaska across the Arctic coast of Canada to Greenland that was completed in 1957. The United States paid the entire cost of the project, more than $500 million, but Canadian contractors were employed where possible, and the Canadians had the right to inspect it. Clauses in the enabling agreement protected the environment and the Native people. Farther south, along the 55th parallel, the Canadian government spent $200 million to build the 'mid-Canada line', a largely automated string of radar stations, to serve as a back-up, and along the Canadian–American border the 'Pinetree line', an additional back-up.

Forty-one of the DEW line stations were built in Canada; the four largest, at Cape Dyer, Hall Beach, Cambridge Bay, and Cape Perry, each had a complement of forty military and civilian personnel. Depending on their sites, the auxiliary stations were staffed by five to twenty-five men. The construction of these facilities resembled the construction of the Alaska Highway, though it involved a much wider area and more difficult conditions. As many as 200,000 tonnes of material and supplies had to be transported north each year in the mid-1950s, and nearly 20,000 workers were employed on the various sites. The project was a bonanza for air freight carriers and Canadian suppliers.

Whatever the geopolitical value of the DEW line, it brought dramatic changes to large areas of the Northwest Territories. The many airfields and landing strips built for the construction and maintenance of the stations brought modern air service to the region. Moreover, when the construction period ended, roughly a thousand employees remained to operate the stations. A hundred of these were Inuit, and the DEW line proved a powerful magnet, drawing Inuit families to work either temporarily in construction or permanently in service occupations.

Another military presence in the NWT was the Strategic Air Command (SAC) base at Frobisher Bay (Iqaluit), complementing the one at Goose Bay, Labrador. The purpose of SAC was to be ready at all times to deliver 'massive retaliation' to the USSR in case of attack. B-52 bombers loaded with nuclear bombs flew

Mark Kalluak, language co-ordinator, Eskimo Point, 1988. NWT Government photo.

between these and similar bases in the United States twenty-four hours a day. Forty years later it is difficult to appreciate the fears of an age when it was commonly believed that the earth would be a glowing ember before 1970; the *zeitgeist* was brilliantly reflected in the film *Dr. Strangelove*. In this climate of fear, Canada was not inclined to quarrel with the American perceptions of the world (politicians who were so inclined, including John Diefenbaker, found their careers blighted), and any suggestions that the DEW line and the other installations were harming the Canadian North or its people were dismissed as the whining of 'peaceniks'.

The great irony of the DEW line and its ancillary facilities is that despite their great cost—easily a billion dollars in all—they were redundant almost as soon as they were finished. The development of intercontinental ballistic missiles, which could cross the Arctic in minutes rather than hours, and satellites that could instantly detect the launch of a missile, made most of the radar facilities obsolete. In the end, the technology that really posed a danger to both America and the USSR proved to be nuclear-powered submarines carrying missiles with multiple warheads; capable of sneaking close to the target country, these were extremely hard to detect. The defence against missiles, developed in the 1960s, was other missiles, and these were located mostly in places such as North Dakota rather than the Arctic. Quite early in the Cold War it became obvious that there would never be a traditional land invasion of the North, and most of the Canadian defence presence in the region was abandoned in the 1960s, except for a small defence headquarters in Yellowknife. The North became a testing ground for Cruise missiles in particular, which were regularly sent down the Mackenzie Valley in preparation for Siberian conditions. When the Soviet economy eventually collapsed in the late 1980s, defence expenditures in the North became even more difficult to justify.

Spending on civilian projects, however, began to increase as the federal government concentrated its attention on the North in a number of new and innovative ways. A good example of the change in government attitude is the history of Dawson City in the post-war era. When the Alaska Highway bypassed the old territorial capital, its pre-eminence was lost, and in 1953 the government moved to Whitehorse. In 1955 a road was finally opened to the town, but it came too late, and in killing off the river steamboats it struck another blow to the local economy. When the last dredge ceased operations in 1964, Dawson City seemed doomed to be a ghost town. Just in time, however, it was reborn, this time as a tourist attraction.

The phoenix-like rebirth of Dawson City from the ashes of the gold-mining economy is one of the more interesting stories of the modern North, though it replays a very old theme—the North as the object of the plans and enthusiasms of outsiders. A foretaste of the transformation of the northern Yukon occurred in 1955, when the Quaker Oats Company, sponsors of a popular radio show featuring Sergeant Preston of the Mounted Police and his dog King, launched a promotional campaign to increased the sales of its Puffed Wheat. The company's advertising agency bought 19 acres of land near Dawson City, printed fancifully decorated deeds to it, and announced that, for a 'limited time only', each box of the cereal would contain a deed to one square inch of the Klondike gold fields. It was one of the most successful sales promotions in North American history; within a few weeks 21 million boxes containing deeds were sold. The people who held the deeds actually owned nothing; they were never formally registered, and the Yukon government repossessed the land in 1965 for non-payment of taxes. Yet the stunt had tapped a deep vein of advertising gold, and tourists for years afterwards drove the land office and the staff of the Yukon Archives to distraction by producing their certificates and asking to see their square inch of the Klondike.

The Quaker Oats campaign was an early indication of the Yukon's new role as a kind of historical theme park—a northern Upper Canada Village or Williamsburg, Virginia. Another was the publication in 1957 of Pierre Berton's *Klondike*, a popular evocation of the gold-rush era sixty years before. The book sold well both in Canada and in the United States, and revived interest in the episode. It also stimulated a desperate attempt by Dawson City to save itself. The difficulty lay in persuading enough tourists travelling the Alaska Highway to make the long detour to the town to see the few attractions it could offer—Robert Service's cabin, a museum, a partly derelict Palace Grand Theatre, and a few decaying buildings from the turn of the century. Fortunately, the federal government was disposed to spend money on historical restorations in the North—something that would have been inconceivable a generation earlier—and when Dawson City's boosters approached Ottawa in 1962 with an idea for a festival to be held two years later, their plan was accepted.

The result was the Dawson Gold Rush Festival of 1964, the centrepiece of which was a musical theatre production put on by a professional troupe. The whole festival cost the federal government $1.6 million, but 18,000 tourists—twice the usual summer number—came north, and they spent $1.9 million in town. Although the festival was not a total success, it pointed the way to the future. In 1967 the Historic Sites and Monuments Board of Canada recommended that Dawson City be made a National Historic Site, and the government began to pour the first of many millions into the restoration of the Palace Grand, the ss *Keno* (one of the old steamboats; the ss *Klondike* was restored at Whitehorse), many of the town's buildings, and eventually the derelict gold dredge that had settled into the mud of Bonanza Creek.

CHAPTER TEN

Search for a Future:
The Modern North, 1970-1995

The history of the Canadian North in the past quarter-century has been dominated by two issues, the first old and the second relatively new: the search for resource wealth, and the increasing assertiveness and power of the First Nations of the two territories. Both have worked changes in the Yukon and the Northwest Territories that none but visionaries could have imagined a generation earlier.

The resources that dominated the era were gas and oil. In the early 1970s, after twenty-five years of prosperity and rising energy consumption in the industrialized world, the predictions of conservationists and 'doomsayers' began to come true: the United States had ceased to be a net exporter of petroleum and had instead become dependent on imported oil; the Organization of Petroleum Exporting Countries (OPEC) discovered its power; and there was an 'energy crisis' (the quotation marks appear in deference to the lingering suspicion that it was artificially created to enrich the oil companies). In 1974 there were actual shortages of gasoline in some places, with accompanying public disorders, and the price per gallon, which had remained at roughly forty cents since the end of

the war, began to rise, eventually increasing sixfold. Most of the reserves of natural gas and petroleum south of the 60th parallel had long since been discovered, and many were largely depleted. The solution, much touted in the 1970s but largely ignored since, was a new ethic of conservation, and the increased price of energy forced the implementation of a number of long-overdue measures, such as the development of more fuel-efficient automobiles. Happily for the wasteful North American way of life, however, there was an alternative to conservation: just before the crisis began, huge new finds had been made in the Canadian and the American Arctic.

In 1968 it was announced that a discovery had been made in Prudhoe Bay, off the north coast of Alaska, amounting to ten billion barrels of oil and twenty-five trillion cubic feet of natural gas. The Arctic Ocean in that region was shallow enough to permit extraction by means of stationary platforms not far from shore, and the only question was how the oil would be brought to market (the gas wells were capped for later use). The American answer was to build the Alyeska pipeline 1,270 kilometres

Future prime minister Jean Chrétien, then minister of Indian Affairs, arriving at Iqaluit, August 1969. NWT Archives, Smith Collection, N91-028:0122.

from the north coast to the south at Prince William Sound, a project that cost $7.7 billion, and when finished in 1977 delivered over a million barrels a day to southern consumers. The pipeline was tremendously controversial. It opponents predicted that there would be breaks in the line, and that oil spills would devastate the fragile environment of the Alaskan tundra. As it happens, most of the environmental damage caused by the shipment of oil has occurred at sea rather than in Alaska itself. The project did pour large sums of money into the state's economy; Alaska's revenues from royalties on the oil were $10,000 per capita in 1981, and in the next year totalled $3.5 billion. Alaska abolished its state income tax, built hundreds of public facilities, including a high school in every hamlet in the state, and began to pay each resident a 'dividend' of $1,000 per year.

In the Canadian North, meanwhile, there was much exploration but little actual production. The Trudeau government used tax incentives to encourage exploration in the Beaufort Sea, north of the Yukon and the Mackenzie Delta, by a number of companies, particularly Dome Petroleum, though Esso, Shell, and Petro-Canada were also active. By 1976 Imperial Oil alone had spent more than $500

High-rise building under construction, Iqaluit, August 1969. NWT Archives, Smith Collection, N91-028:0124.

million in Arctic exploration and drilling. The initial estimate of reserves in the Beaufort Sea was six billion barrels of oil, worth $150 billion in the late 1970s (twice that if oil went to $50 per barrel, as many predicted it would), and ninety trillion cubic feet of gas. Additional discoveries were made farther north, in the islands of the high Arctic, though it was difficult to say how oil and gas from wells in the region might be brought to market. Nevertheless, with a seemingly insatiable market, a huge supply, a compliant government, and a public resigned to ever-rising prices, there seemed to be no reason it could not be done.

The result was a proposal for the largest mega-project ever proposed for northern Canada, and one of the most widely publicized controversies ever to arise in the region. The project was the Mackenzie Valley pipeline, designed to carry natural gas and eventually oil from the Arctic Ocean up the Mackenzie River Valley to the North American network in Alberta, with a spur running west along the Arctic coast to the American fields at Prudhoe Bay. Stretching 3,860 kilometres, it would be the longest in the world. Rival companies combined to form a consortium, Canadian Arctic Gas Pipeline Ltd, which in March 1974 applied to the National

Actor reciting Robert Service's poetry to a group of tourists outside the poet's cabin, Dawson City. Yukon Government photo.

Energy Board for permission to begin construction.

If this permission had been sought in 1944 or 1954, it would undoubtedly have been granted without much fuss. But in 1974 the project ran into two strong and fiercely determined sources of opposition: the environmental movement and the emerging strength of the northern First Nations. The federal government's response to the application for approval was to set up a royal commission of inquiry headed by Thomas Berger, a justice of the Supreme Court of British Columbia. Berger, described in *The Canadian Encyclopedia* as 'lawyer, judge, humanitarian', was a man of well-known liberal sym-

pathies, and the government that appointed him presumably knew that his commission would be the opposite of a rubber stamp. The commission's hearings began in the spring of 1975, and dealt as expected with thousands of pages of technical data and analysis. The project was unprecedented; twice as long as the Alyeska pipeline in Alaska (which in any case carried oil, not gas), it would run across the Yukon coastal plain, an area of extreme environmental sensitivity, and would rely on some untried technology. Much of it would run through permafrost, which would melt with disastrous results if disturbed (the solution for that was to refrigerate

Pottery workshop, Rankin Inlet, 1967, part of the tremendous contemporary renaissance of Inuit art. NWT Archives, Smith Collection, N91-028:0150.

the gas) and there were other technical questions to which the consortium found it difficult to give plausible answers.

What made the commission one of the most important public events of the decade, however, was the manner in which Berger's commission dealt with the fears and the complaints of the First Nations people—the Dene, Inuit, and Métis of the Mackenzie district—that the pipeline would destroy their land and their way of life. Rather than hold the hearings in some large southern city, Berger took his commission on the road in the North, visiting thirty-five communities and listening to a thousand witnesses. The opposition from the Native people was heartfelt and intense. They feared that construction of the pipeline would ruin their traplines, prevent the caribou from breeding, corrupt their communities, poison their fishing streams, and bring every kind of evil upon them. That all these things had already happened to a greater or lesser degree during the construction of the Alaska Highway lent weight to their fears. When they spoke of their feelings for the land, there was no doubt that the Dene spoke from the heart:

Louis Caesar of Fort Good Hope: This land it is just like our blood because we live off the animals that feed off the land.

Georgina Tabac of Fort Good Hope: Every time the white people . . . start tearing up our land, I feel as if they are cutting our own flesh, because that is the way we feel about the land. It is our flesh.

Susie Tutcho of Fort Franklin: My father really loved this land, and we love our land. The grass and trees are our flesh, the animals are our flesh.

Marie Moosenose of Lac La Martre: We love our land because we survive with it. It gives us life, the land gives us life.[1]

A strong voice for the Dene was Father René Fumoleau, whose book *As Long as This Land Shall Last: A History of Treaty 8 and Treaty 11, 1870–1939*, published in 1973,[2] provided a historical background that was of crucial importance to the Dene in the early stages of the pipeline controversy and their land claim. The hearings in the Mackenzie Valley communities, widely publicized on television, culminated in the publication of *Northern Frontier, Northern Homeland: Report of the Mackenzie Valley Pipeline Inquiry* (1977); unusually for a royal commission document, it was full of photographs and eloquent quotations from First Nations speakers, and soon became a bestseller.

Northern Frontier, Northern Homeland was required reading in university courses in Native Studies, not only because the issue it dealt with was so important, but because Berger permitted the witnesses to speak on a range of social matters that had little to do

with the issue at hand, yet everything to do with the social injustice that the Dene people felt. A man named Dolphus Shea, for instance, testifying at Fort Franklin, recounted his experiences in a residential school at Aklavik:

When we got there we were told that if we spoke Indian they would whip us until our hands were blue on both sides. And also we were told that the Indian religion was superstitious and pagan. . . . The first day we got to school all our clothes were taken away . . . and everybody got a haircut which was a bald haircut. We all felt lost and wanted to go home, and some cried for weeks and weeks. . . . Today, I think back on the hostel life and I feel ferocious.[3]

It came as no surprise when the commission's report recommended that no pipeline be built for ten years, until the land claims of the indigenous people were settled and further study and planning had been carried out; the government swiftly adopted this recommendation. Those on the losing side of the issue complained that the commission was not unbiased: Berger had hired as an adviser Mel Watkins, a political economist best known for forming the 'Waffle Group', a left-wing splinter faction of the New Democratic Party, and no friend of multinational corporations. They also suggested that the Dene did not speak for all northerners, and indeed a significant number of northerners, some of them Native (especially Métis), were bitterly disappointed when their dreams of economic development evaporated.

A second and equally interesting, though less publicized, inquiry of a similar sort was held at about the same time. It concerned a

John Munro, minister of Indian Affairs, and Peter Green, of the Committee on Original People's Entitlement (COPE), signing the Inuvialuit comprehensive claims agreement at Inuvik, May 1984. *News of the North* photo.

proposal for a gas pipeline to run from the Canadian and American fields across the Yukon to the Alaska Highway and thence to southern markets. Because much of this line would run along an existing development corridor, the arguments against it were not as strong as in the Mackenzie Valley. The proponent of this project was Foothills Pipe Lines of Calgary, headed by Bob Blair of Calgary. As an all-Canadian company, it grated less on the sensibilities of Canadian nationalists. This proposal too led to a royal commission, headed by Kenneth Lysyk, Dean of Law at the University of British Columbia, which held hearings in

the summer of 1977, and which also recommended a moratorium until Native land claims had been settled. In this case, however, the government decided to press ahead, and enabling legislation was passed in Ottawa and Whitehorse. Construction, planned to begin in 1981, promised a new bonanza for the Yukon. Unfortunately for the developers, though, by that time the bloom was off the energy crisis. Cost estimates for the project initially came in at $4.4 billion; by 1982 they had reached $15 billion, a sum at which the bankers balked. In 1983 the company closed its office in Whitehorse and the dream was over. Whether

Sonny Lindner, winner of Quest '84, with his team on the Yukon River. Yukon Government photo.

the project will be revived in the foreseeable future is questionable, given the discovery of large new gas fields in the Peace River district of northern BC that can easily be connected to the North American pipeline system.

A powerful factor in the defeat of both these megaprojects was the growing strength of the First Nations of the Yukon and Northwest Territories—surely the most significant development in the Canadian North since the end of the Second World War. Before 1970 the First Nations had not been part of the political equation in northern Canada; the region's development was planned and executed by non-Natives who, far from consulting

them, scarcely took their interests into consideration. But by 1980 the First Nations were playing a key role in northern politics and development, and it had become unthinkable to exclude them from any process of importance to the two territories. There were several reasons for this remarkable change. One was the increased social awareness and activism of the 1960s and 1970s, in which racism, sexism, and paternalism all became officially unfashionable, and the empowerment of the previously powerless became a goal among influential segments of society. Another was the rising levels of education among the Native people themselves. Whatever may be said of the

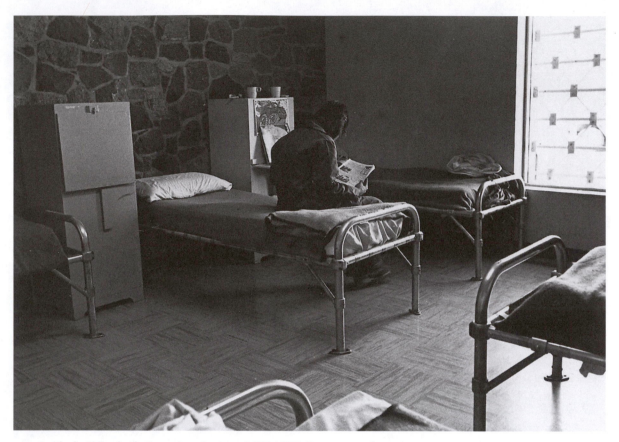

Inside the Yellowknife Corrections Institute, 1977. NWT Government photo.

schooling inflicted upon these people after the war, it did produce a growing educated élite, and the first Native university graduates, trained in the law and other professions, served as powerful advocates for their people's interests. The growth of liberal social attitudes among the middle class, fostered by the tremendous increase in the proportion of the population going to university after 1945 and carried forward by the 'baby boomers', made social justice, however one might define it, a watchword of the era.

A mark of the changes taking place in the Canadian North was the increasing devolution of political power to the region. As late as 1970, both territories were governed by councils made up of appointed and elected members and headed by commissioners appointed by the federal government with the power to veto legislation. Since most of the territorial revenues came from Ottawa in the form of direct grants and other payments, the government had tremendous power over local affairs. Although the Yukon had enjoyed a considerable measure of control over local affairs since the end of the gold rush, the NWT was ruled in large matters and small by absentees; only in 1967 was the territorial capital moved to Yellowknife, after a few years in Fort Smith. In the 1970s, however, the two territories moved rapidly along the road to self-government, though by different routes. In the Yukon, party politics was introduced to the Council when the territorial Conservative Party won a majority of the elected seats and formed a cabinet in 1977. In 1978 the federal government accepted the idea that the territorial commissioner should become a figurehead, accepting the advice of the elected council. Responsible government in the Canadian sense—that the Crown is the servant of the people rather than their master—had come to the Canadian North.

In the NWT the evolution of local autonomy proceeded along a somewhat different path. In 1970 the Territorial Council consisted of ten elected and four appointed members. In 1975 its membership was expanded to fifteen, all elected, and in 1979 to twenty-two. In the 1975 territorial elections, nine of the fifteen were of First Nations descent, and in 1979 fourteen of the twenty-two. What makes the NWT's political system unique, however, is not only the fact that the Legislative Assembly, as it came to be called, has a majority of Native members. More noteworthy is the absence of political parties. Members are elected because of their local status or popularity, not because of party affiliation, and although there is an administration that forms a government, it has no assurance that its measures will win a majority. Rather, it must seek consensus, which requires that the measures it proposes be moderate and widely acceptable. This tradition, which has weathered an unsuccessful attempt by the New Democratic Party to introduce party politics, makes it difficult for any one person to acquire power, and makes railroading of

Tony Penikett, elected Yukon government leader in 1985. Yukon Government photo.

legislation, against the wishes of a determined sector of opinion, almost impossible.

For the Native people of the North, as elsewhere in Canada, the defining moment, the 'firebell in the night', to quote Jefferson's description of the Missouri Compromise on slavery, was the Trudeau government's assimilationist White Paper of 1969, which envisaged the abolition of reserves and the absorption of Native people into the Canadian mainstream. Though the paper itself was hastily abandoned, the outcry against it served as a call to action. The vehicle through which this outcry

Thomas Berger (with suit and tie) and a group of news reporters representing five languages, at Yellowknife during the pipeline hearings, 1976. NWT Government photo.

was transformed into political strength for the First Nations was the energy crisis of the early 1970s, and the first northern movement towards this transformation came from the village of Old Crow in the Yukon, where geological research connected with oil and gas exploration was under way. Early in 1972 the Indians of Old Crow presented a petition to the House of Commons asking it to stop this research, fearful that the seismic activities associated with it would damage the environment and interfere with the life cycle of the caribou.

This protest became part of a general land claim brought forward in 1973 by the Yukon Native Brotherhood (later the Council for Yukon Indians) in a document entitled 'Together Today for our Children Tomorrow'. This was the first 'comprehensive' claim in the Canadian North. Claims negotiated between First Nations and the Canadian government in recent years have fallen into two categories, specific and comprehensive. Specific claims arise out of problems with interpretation or implementation of treaties; typically, a band will complain that some of its reserve was taken for a road or other purpose without compensation. Comprehensive claims are negotiated in areas where treaties were never signed, and involve allocation of land and cash payments, among other arrangements;

Suzie Koaha posing in the Cambridge Bay Co-op store, 1988. NWT Government photo.

they are essentially modern versions of the treaties signed in the nineteenth century. Because most of the North is not covered by the treaties—the exception is Treaty 11, signed in the Mackenzie Valley in 1921, the provisions of which were never fully implemented—the first six comprehensive claims were all in the territories and northern Quebec.

It is part of the British-Canadian legal tradition in regard to indigenous people that they must be compensated for their rights to the land before it can be sold to private interests or developed. In law, the Native people do not 'own' the land; rather they have rights to it ('usufructuary' rights, meaning the right to use it) that must be dealt with. This is why the

government has usually negotiated treaties at the beginning of settlement by newcomers.

When the first post-Confederation treaties were made with the Indians of the Prairies, beginning with Treaty 1, signed in 1871 outside the walls of Lower Fort Garry in Manitoba, the Native signers were weak and demoralized; they may also have been deceived by the government negotiators as to the implications of the documents. The result was that they traded their Aboriginal rights to the land for small parcels of land—the reserves—small annuities, and a few other gifts from the government. A century later, by contrast, the First Nations of northern Canada were well aware of the value of their land; they

HRH Prince Charles being presented with a bead belt by Chief Johnny Charlie of Fort McPherson at the opening of the Prince of Wales Northern Heritage Centre in Yellowknife, 1979. NWT Government photo.

had educated members of their people to speak for them, and they had found many vocal allies among the non-Native population. Though most realized that a settlement of their claims was inevitable, everyone knew that the price would be very high.

The Yukon Native Brotherhood's claim resulted in a good deal of friction and misunderstanding between Natives and non-Natives in the territory. Some non-Natives, alarmed by extreme statements on the part of people tasting political power for the first time, began to

fear—or pretended to fear—that the Native people were planning to lay claim to the city of Whitehorse, together with all the infrastructure that had been built up in the territory since the gold rush. It was galling to the non-Native Yukoners that they were not participants in the negotiations. Since these were legally a matter between the federal government and the Native people, the Yukon government was not included; at first it did not even have observer status in meetings. As negotiations proceeded, however, it became apparent that the Council for Yukon Indians had no intention of turning back history, or of seizing all that newcomers had built in the territory over a century. The realization that payment for loss of Aboriginal rights would come from the federal government, whose responsibility the matter was, and would result in the funnelling of many millions of dollars into the territory, opened a new perspective on the matter.

Negotiations dragged on for years. Though a draft agreement in principle was approved by negotiators for both sides, it was rejected by the Native communities. The sticking point was in part the principle of 'extinguishment': the government wanted Aboriginal rights extinguished over the larger part of the territory, reserving actual ownership and use for certain designated sections, so that the claims, once settled, could never be resurrected. The thought of surrendering claim to any of the Yukon, which had once all been theirs, was very difficult for many of the First Nations people, and negotiators who counselled compromise were sometimes repudiated as having sold out to the government. Negotiations proceeded fitfully throughout the 1970s and 1980s, helped along by the sympa-

The Babbage River, flowing through the Yukon's North Slope to the Beaufort Sea. Fred Bruemmer photo. VF 1343.

Near the treeline in the Ogilvie Mountains, Yukon. Fred Bruemmer photo. TF 1996.

Yukon forest and mountains along the road to Haines, Alaska. Fred Bruemmer photo. TF 1638.

The ubiquitous fireweed, the Yukon's floral emblem, flourishing along the Dempster Highway. Fred Bruemmer photo. TF 1782.

Pauta Saila (1916–). `Owl', 1964. Printed by Echalook Pingwartok (1942). Stonecut. Collection of the West Baffin Eskimo Co-operative Ltd, on loan to the McMichael Canadian Art Collection.

Parr (1893–1969). 'Walrus Hunters on Sea Ice', 1967. Printed by Eegyvudluk Pootoogook (1931). Stonecut. Collection of the West Baffin Eskimo Co-operative Ltd, on loan to the McMichael Canadian Art Collection.

thetic attitude of a social-democratic administration in the Yukon elected in 1985 and headed by Tony Penikett, and by the fact that the federal government eventually brought the territorial government into the negotiating process. As of the summer of 1997, however, the matter is still not entirely resolved: an agreement has been worked out, but some of the First Nations communities still have not agreed to it.

The most dramatic of the comprehensive claims was that of the Dene and Métis of the Mackenzie Valley. In 1921 they had signed a treaty urged upon them by the government at the time of oil discoveries at Norman Wells. Unlike those who signed the treaties of the 1870s, a number of witnesses to the treaty signing of 1921 survived to testify before the Berger commission that they had been lied to and that the treaty had been misrepresented to them. Because the promised reserves had never been laid out—when the oil boom at Norman Wells fizzled, the government lost interest in the treaty—Ottawa decided to consider the original document a nullity and start over again with negotiations. The First Nations of the region were in a strong position to assert their rights, for the entire question of comprehensive claims in northern Canada arose at the same time as the proposal for the Mackenzie Valley pipeline, and their claims would have to be dealt with before any construction could proceed.

In the summer of 1975, in the midst of the Berger Commission hearings, the Dene issued the 'Dene Declaration', a forceful manifesto that brought their position to national attention. Probably the most radical document issued by a major Native organization to that time, it began, 'We the Dene of the N.W.T.

Lillian Shamee and her son Clifford, Eskimo Point, 1988. NWT Government photo.

insist on the right to be regarded by ourselves and the world as a nation', and went on:

The government of Canada is not the government of the Dene. The Government of the N.W.T. is not the government of the Dene. . . . [Although] there are realities we are forced to submit to, such as the existence of a country called Canada, we insist on the right to self-determination as a distinct people. . . . We the Dene are part of the Fourth World. . . . What we seek then is independence and self-determination within the country of Canada.

Although the Dene leaders insisted that the declaration was not a separatist document, it was denounced as such by Judd Buchanan, minister of Indian Affairs, and a debate ensued in the press as to whether the Dene really meant what they said or the declaration was simply a tactic. The Dene later expanded on the declaration in a document entitled 'Recognition of the Dene Nation through Dene government', in which a number of powers of 'provincial-like' jurisdiction were listed. Among them were a 'provincial equivalent which would be the replacement of the existing territorial government', the 'power to set up a system of Dene law in non-criminal matters', indirect and resource taxation, the 'power to start and control a bank', education, immigration, the right to make certain agreements with foreign governments, and interprovincial and international trade with other First Nations, among others. The only significant powers that this document did not claim were the rights to run the army and the post office. The arrangement was much like what René Lévesque would later call 'sovereignty-association', and the federal government, eternally embroiled with Quebec's nationalist aspirations, viewed it with alarm.

The comprehensive claim of the First Nations of the Mackenzie Valley has followed a difficult path, and is currently even farther from resolution than the Yukon claim. The problem was partly what was perceived as the intransigence of the Dene, which led the government at one point to cut off the funding that had been provided to help them work on their case. A further difficulty was that the First Nations were not united; the Métis, more inclined to accommodation, eventually decid-ed to negotiate a separate agreement. Subsequently the Dene also became divided, and the different Dene First Nations are now negotiating separately as well.

A third land claim north of 60 was that of the Inuvialuit, the Inuit of the western Arctic, who in the early 1970s organized themselves as the Committee for Original People's Entitlement, or COPE. The Inuvialuit, who numbered about 2,500 at that time, live in the Mackenzie Delta–Beaufort Sea region in the communities of Aklavik, Inuvik, Tuktoyaktuk, Sachs Harbour, Paulatuk, and Holman Island. For reasons involving the internal dynamics of the different First Nations, their claim was settled relatively quickly. The Inuvialuit had four distinct goals: to preserve a land base for their traditional activities, to preserve their cultural identity, to have a voice in the changes that were overtaking their world, and to be compensated for the surrender of their rights. This claim was the first in the two territories to be settled; under its terms the Inuvialuit retained ownership of the sub-surface mineral rights to about 13,000 square kilometres of land, more limited rights to 95,000 km² (about half their original lands), substantial cash payments spread out over a number of years, and royalties from resources, among other benefits.

The fourth comprehensive claim in the Territories was that of the 15,000 Inuit of the central and eastern Arctic. The Nunavut ('our land') claim was presented early in 1976 by the Inuit Tapirisat ('brotherhood'), and had as its main demand the creation of a separate territory, to be called Nunavut. The history of the people of Nunavut is one of astonishingly rapid transformation. Before 1940, they were largely ignored by the outside world, including

Nunavut

the government; it was only in 1939 that Ottawa assumed any formal responsibility for their welfare. Very few had any formal education, they were seriously affected by tuberculosis and other diseases, and the fur trade, a staple of their economy, was declining. Yet they had one strength that no other Native group in Canada possessed: they constituted the major-

ity of the population of their land. The Yukon Indians make up about a third of the population of that territory, and in the Mackenzie Valley the Dene and Métis are outnumbered by non-Natives, but the Inuit are a strong majority in the central and eastern Arctic. This meant that as soon as they were able to seize the levers of political power, they could control

Martha Black (1866–1957), first lady of the Yukon and the second woman elected to the House of Commons. NAC, C81812.

their destiny to an unparalleled degree.

An early indication of this power was the renaming of Frobisher Bay, the administrative centre of the eastern Arctic, as Iqaluit. The greatest proof, however, was the success of their campaign to divide the Northwest Territories in two, with Nunavut in the east under their control, leaving the Mackenzie district to a less certain future. The division of the NWT had considerable logic behind it, since in effect the territory was simply what was left over from all the other political jurisdictions in

Canada: after British Columbia and the Prairie provinces had their northern boundaries arbitrarily fixed at 60° north, after Quebec had been extended north to Ungava and Ontario to James Bay, and after the western section had been set aside as the Yukon, what was left was the Northwest Territories. So long as Ottawa dominated the NWT, all sections were equally powerless, but when the territorial government began to have real authority, the cultural distances between the eastern section, centred in Iqaluit, and the western section, centred 2,100 kilometres away in the capital at Yellowknife, became increasingly apparent, and partition, strongly favoured in the east, became inevitable. Planning for it is underway as these words are being written.

As we have seen, the modern political history of the Canadian North—the period in which the two territories became largely self-governing—stretches back barely twenty years in the Yukon, and in the Northwest Territories less than that. Nevertheless, several northern political figures achieved national prominence in those years.

The Yukon has had a member of Parliament since 1902. Until 1962, its member also represented the western, or Mackenzie, district of the Northwest Territories, while the rest of the NWT had no political representation at all. In 1962 the NWT was given a seat and the franchise was extended over the whole territory; the North thus had two seats until 1976, when in a preview of the current partition, the NWT constituency was split in two. Ethel Blondin-Andrew has been the member of Parliament for the Western Arctic since 1988, and was appointed a junior cabinet member—Secretary of State for Training and Youth—in

Pope John Paul II and Dene leaders, Fort Simpson, 1987. NWT Government photo.

the 1993 Chrétien government. Both of the territory's constituencies are represented by members of First Nations; in the eastern constituency, originally Nunatsiaq, now renamed Nunavut, this has been true since its establishment. It is, as well, the largest constituency in Canada, and the one with the largest percentage of Aboriginal constituents: 75 per cent are Inuit. It is currently represented by Nancy Karetak-Lindell.

For all but nine of the years between 1902 and 1988, the Yukon seat was held by Conservatives. George and Martha Black between them held it from 1921 until 1949. Both were

vigorous partisans; he was Speaker of the House in the government of R.B. Bennett, and in 1935 she became the second woman ever to be elected to Parliament (Agnes Macphail was the first, in 1921), running for her husband's seat when he suffered a nervous breakdown. From 1957 to 1987 the Yukon was represented by Erik Nielsen, an even more partisan Conservative, who had come to the territory in 1952 to practise law, eventually becoming deputy prime minister and minister of Defence in the first Mulroney administration. His memoirs, which tell more about the national politics of the era than about the North, are remarkably frank and unsentimental about the public figures of his day, and unusually candid about his own shortcomings.[4]

Nielsen can be seen as a traditional northern figure—like George Black, he was a man who came north for economic reasons and became a successful politician of a very conservative stripe. Very different, though just as northern, was his successor, Audrey McLaughlin, who was the Yukon's member of Parliament from 1988 until 1997, and leader of the federal New Democratic Party from 1989 to 1995. A strongly committed social democrat, she came to the Yukon in 1979 for one of the oldest and one of the newest reasons—to find herself and get a fresh start in life:

> *I like my job and enjoyed the city [Toronto], but I didn't want to get too comfortable. . . . My few possessions were beginning to feel like so many nails in my coffin, and I realized I wanted to take the lid off—to cut free. . . . There were two options. Either I would go to the University of Toronto School of Medicine and try for a Ph.D. in community health planning . . . or I would follow a long-held dream and head for the North. . . . in the end, the lure of the North won out: I decided that the Yukon would be my Ph.D.[5]*

When she retired from politics in 1997 she was succeeded by Louise Hardy, another member of the NDP. As the leader of a major political party, McLaughlin, even more than Nielsen, was seen as a national rather than a northern figure. Nevertheless, both did attract attention to the region; Nielsen's nickname, 'Yukon Erik', reminded Canadians where he came from.

In the summer of 1997, one of the North's oldest industries is experiencing a revival. New gold-mining ventures are being developed in the old gold fields near Dawson City, and a new and spectacularly valuable enterprise is well under way in the Northwest Territories. Three hundred kilometres northeast of Yellowknife, Jacques Cartier's *diamants du Canada* seem at last to be a reality, for at the Lac de Gras site, the Blackwater Group and Broken Hill Properties are developing the first diamond mine in North America. Five diamond-bearing kimberlite pipes will be excavated over a 25-year period in an operation that will involve draining five lakes and filling a sixth with tailings. These mines will be the largest industrial employer in the NWT, and are expected to produce $12 billion worth of diamonds and generate $2.5 billion in revenue for the territorial and federal governments. More than 800 jobs per year, on average, will be generated, many of them employing local people, which will reduce the territorial unemployment rate by 3 per cent once the mines are in operation.

As Canada approaches the year 2000, its future seems to be in a state of permanent uncertainty. Nothing is certain in the North either, except that its future will be different from its past. It may not become wealthy, or even self-sufficient—it will probably continue to consume more public funds per capita than any other jurisdiction in Canada. What is most remarkable about the North at the end of the twentieth century, however, and what the gold miners, missionaries, traders, Mounted Policemen, and even the Native leaders of the past would find most astonishing, is the tremendous power and influence of the First Nations in the region. Less than fifty years ago, the northern First Nations were marginalized in their own country; yet today the North has truly become, in the words of the Berger report, a 'Northern Homeland' for First Nations.

The best evidence of this transformation is the way Native culture has been preserved and enhanced. In the case of Native languages, the preservation began none too soon. Much has been lost in this century, including an entire language—Angela Sidney, who died in 1991, was the last living speaker of Tagish. Once there was general agreement on the need for cultural preservation, however, progress was rapid. One of the offshoots of the comprehensive claims process was an increase in the attention paid to language preservation, instruction, and enhancement. In 1973, for instance, the Inuit Tapirisat established the Inuit Cultural Institute at Eskimo Point to translate materials from English to Inuktitut, compile a dialect dictionary, collect the stories of elders, invent new words for the technologies that were penetrating the land, and develop a school curriculum that would respect the indigenous culture. By the early 1980s, schools in Inuit communities were providing instruction in Inuktitut at the elementary level. In 1986 an Inuit language centre was established at Tuktoyaktuk, and Dene language centres at Fort Franklin and Fort Simpson were set up around the same time. The Legislative Council of the NWT, where as late as 1967 only English and occasionally French were spoken, now boasts simultaneous translation into seven languages: English, Inuktitut, and five languages spoken by the Dene. In 1980 the Igloolik Education Society began taking groups of

Fly-in fishing in a remote Yukon lake. Yukon Government photo.

teenagers to hunting camps, where they were taught traditional hunting and survival skills. And some families on Baffin Island began to spend part of the year in outpost camps, believing that cultural survival was as important to their children as formal schooling.

The economic future of the Yukon and the

Northwest Territories (or the Yukon, Nunavut, and Denendeh, as the Dene would like to call their portion of the NWT) is uncertain, as it always has been. Resource industries and government largesse make notoriously unstable economic bases, and the current program of financial stringency in Ottawa does not augur well for the continuation of the generous support the region has enjoyed in the past. But the North has always see-sawed between financial feasts and famines. One year the mines at Pine Point close down because of low world prices for lead and zinc; the next year there is an exploration and staking boom when diamond-bearing rocks are found near the mouth of the Coppermine River on the Arctic coast. One year the mine at Faro, an economic mainstay of the Yukon, is open, employing hundreds of people at union wages; the next year it closes and some months later it reopens, paying much lower wages to non-union workers. There is no certainty or stability in any of this activity. The only constant is the people, particularly the Native people. Governments, traders, missionaries, teachers—these come and go, but for the Native people, as well as an increasing number of non-Natives who have committed themselves to the region, the North is a homeland forever.

NOTES

Preface

1. *The Opening of the Canadian North, 1870–1914* (Toronto: McClelland and Stewart, 1971) and *The Northward Expansion of Canada, 1914–1967* (Toronto: McClelland and Stewart, 1988).

2. K.S. Coates, *Canada's Colonies: A History of the Yukon and Northwest Territories* (Toronto: James Lorimer, 1985).

1: Imagination and Reality

1. I.S. Maclaren, 'The Aesthetic Map of the North, 1845–1859', in K.S. Coates and W.R. Morrison, eds, *Interpreting Canada's North: Selected Readings* (Toronto: Copp Clark Pitman, 1989).

2. Carl Berger, *The Sense of Power: Studies in the Ideas of Canadian Imperialism, 1867–1914* (Toronto: University of Toronto Press, 1970), 129–30.

3. Charles Camsell, 'The New North', *Canadian Geographical Journal* 33 (1946).

4. Hugh Keenleyside, 'Recent Developments in the Canadian North', speech given at McMaster University, May 1949, quoted in Shelagh Grant, *Sovereignty or Security?: Government Policy in the Canadian North, 1936–1950* (Vancouver: University of British Columbia Press, 1988), 148. See also H. Keenleyside, 'Recent Developments in the Canadian North', *Canadian Geographical Journal* 39 (1949).

5. On the mid-Canada development corridor, see Richard Rohmer, *The Green North* (Toronto: Maclean-Hunter, 1970).

6. Translated by William Barr (Montreal: Harvest House, 1978).

7. Barry Lopez, *Arctic Dreams: Imagination and Desire in a Northern Landscape* (New York: Scribner, 1986), xxii–xxiii.

8. Jamie Bastedo, *Shield Country: Life and Times of the Oldest Piece of the Planet* (Calgary: Arctic Institute of North America, 1994), 14.

2: First Peoples

1. Angela Sidney, 'How the World Began: The Story of Crow', in J. Cruikshank, *Life Lived Like a Story: Life Stories of Three Yukon Native Elders* (Vancouver: University of British Columbia Press, 1990), 43.

2. Catharine McClellan et al., *Part of the Land, Part of the Water: A History of the Yukon Indians* (Vancouver: Douglas and McIntyre, 1987), 4–5.

3. McClellan et al., 5–6.

4. 'The Original Affluent Society', Chapter 1 of Marshall D. Sahlins, *Stone Age Economics* (New York: Aldine de Gruyter, 1972).

5. James W. VanStone, *Athapaskan Adaptations: Hunters and Fishermen of the Subarctic Forests* (Arlington Heights, IL: Harlan Davidson, 1974), 8.

6. K.S. Coates, *Best Left as Indians: Native–White Relations in the Yukon Territory 1840–1973* (Montreal: McGill-Queen's University Press, 1991).

7. Robert McGhee, *Ancient People of the Arctic*

(Vancouver: University of British Columbia Press, 1996), 62–3. This book is a lucid and beautifully illustrated history of these people and their successors.

8. Quoted in McGhee, 154.
9. Peter Pitseolak and Dorothy Eber, *People From Our Side* (Montreal and Kingston: McGill-Queen's University Press, 1993), 31.
10. Pitseolak and Eber, 33.

3: Newcomers

1. S.E. Morison, *The European Discovery of America: The Northern Voyages A.D. 500–1600* (New York: Oxford University Press, 1971).
2. Morison, 46.

4: Fur Traders and Missionaries

1. Quoted in W.R. Morrison, *Showing the Flag: The Mounted Police and Canadian Sovereignty in the North, 1894–1925* (Vancouver: University of British Columbia Press, 1985), 153.
2. Quoted in K.S. Coates, *Best Left as Indians*, 78. The standard biography of Bompas is H.A. Cody, *An Apostle of the North: Memoirs of the Right Reverend William Carpenter Bompas, D.D.* (Toronto: Musson, 1908).
3. K.S. Coates, 'Send Only Those Who Rise a Peg: Anglican Clergy in the Yukon, 1858–1932', *Journal of the Canadian Church Historical Society* (Summer 1986).
4. John Webster Grant, *Moon of Wintertime: Missionaries and Indians of Canada in Encounter since 1534* (Toronto: University of Toronto Press, 1984), Kerry Abel, 'Of Two Minds: Dene Response to the Mackenzie Missions 1858–1902', in K.S. Coates and W.R. Morrison, eds, *Interpreting Canada's North: Selected Readings* (Toronto: Copp Clark Pitman, 1989), 89.
5. Quoted in Coates, *Best Left as Indians*, 146.
6. K.S. Coates, 'Betwixt and Between: The Anglican Church and the Children of the Carcross (Chooutla) Residential School, 1922–1954', *BC Studies* 64 (Winter 1984–5).
7. Alice French, *My Name Is Masak* (Winnipeg: Peguis Publishers, 1977).

8. See René Fumoleau, *As Long As This Land Shall Last* (Toronto: McClelland and Stewart, 1973).

5: The Age of Exploration

1. Samuel Hearne, *A Journey to the Northern Ocean*, Richard Glover, ed. (Toronto: Macmillan, 1958), 99–101.
2. Lopez, *Arctic Dreams*, 379–80.

6: Eldorado

1. Pierre Berton, *Klondike: The Last Great Gold Rush* (Toronto: McClelland and Stewart, 1972), 17. First published in 1958, this is still the best account of the episode. Berton's *Klondike Quest: A Photographic Essay 1897–1899* (Toronto: McClelland and Stewart, 1983) contains excellent reproductions of some of the best photographs taken of the gold rush.
2. William Ogilvie, *Early Days on the Yukon & The Story of Its Gold Finds* (Ottawa: Thornburn and Abbott, 1913). The miners' meetings have been analysed by Thomas Stone in three articles: 'The Mounties as Vigilantes: Perceptions of Community and the Transformation of Law in the Yukon, 1885–1897', *Law and Society Review* 14, 1 (Fall 1979); 'Atomistic Order and Frontier Violence: Miners and Whalemen in the Nineteenth Century Yukon', *Ethnology* 22 (October 1983); 'Flux and Authority in a Subarctic Society: The Yukon Miners in the Nineteenth Century', *Ethnohistory* 30, 4 (1983).
3. Quoted in K.S. Coates and W.R. Morrison, *Land of the Midnight Sun: A History of the Yukon* (Edmonton: Hurtig, 1988), 80.
4. S.B. Steele, *Forty Years in Canada* (London: Jenkins, 1915), 296.
5. Martha Black, *My Ninety Years* (Anchorage: Alaska Northwest Publishing, 1976), 30. For a more detailed account of her early life, see Martha Black, *My Seventy Years* (London: Thomas Nelson, 1938).
6. Quoted in Berton, *Klondike*, 143–4.

7: Quiet Years

1. Coates, *Best Left as Indians*, 163

2. Report of Joe Tuckwell, an employee of the Pacific Steam Whaling Company, quoted in Coates and Morrison, *Land of the Midnight Sun*, 121.

3. Quoted in Morrison, *Showing the Flag*, 74.

4. *I, Nuligak*, trans. Maurice Metayer (Toronto: Peter Martin, 1966), 29.

5. Quoted in Coates and Morrison, *Land of the Midnight Sun*, 129.

6. Statement of Sinnisiak to the police, 17 May 1916, quoted in Morrison, *Showing the Flag*, 139. The case was extensively covered in the annual report of the Mounted Police for 1916, and in R.G. Moyles, *British Law and Arctic Men* (Saskatoon: Western Producer Prairie Books, 1979).

7. Jim Lotz, *Northern Realities: The Future of Northern Development in Canada* (Toronto: New Press, 1972), 80.

8: Invasion

1. P.S. Barry, *The Canol Project: An Adventure of the U.S. War Department in Canada's Northwest* (Edmonton: published by the author, 1985), 5.

2. Richard Diubaldo, 'The Alaska Highway in Canada–United States Relations', in K.S. Coates, ed., *The Alaska Highway: Papers of the 40th Anniversary Symposium* (Vancouver: University of British Columbia Press, 1985). See also R.J. Diubaldo, 'The Canol Project in Canadian–American Relations', Canadian Historical Association, *Historical Papers*, 1977.

3. Testimony of Joe Jacquot before the Mackenzie Valley Pipeline inquiry, quoted in Coates and Morrison, *The Alaska Highway in World War II: The U.S. Army of Occupation in Canada's Northwest* (Norman: University of Oklahoma Press, 1992), 96.

4. *Edmonton Journal*, 11 July 1944.

9: The New North

1. Frank J. Tester and Peter Kulchyski, *Tammarniit (Mistakes): Inuit Relocation in the Eastern Arctic, 1939–63* (Vancouver: University of British Columbia Press, 1994), 199.

10: Search for a Future

1. In Thomas R. Berger, *Northern Frontier, Northern Homeland: The Report of the Mackenzie Valley Pipeline Inquiry*, vol. I (Ottawa: Supply and Services Canada, 1977). 94.

2. (Toronto: McClelland and Stewart, 1973).

3. In Berger, *Northern Frontier, Northern Homeland*, 90.

4. Erik Nielsen, *The House Is Not a Home* (Toronto: Macmillan, 1989).

5. Audrey McLaughlin, *A Woman's Place: My Life and Politics* (Toronto: Macfarlane Walter & Ross, 1992) 13.

SUGGESTED READINGS

Amundsen, Roald. *The North West Passage*. London: Constable, 1908.

Bastedo, Jamie. *Shield Country: Life and Times of the Oldest Piece of the Planet*. Calgary: Arctic Institute of North America, 1994.

Berger, Thomas. *Northern Frontier/Northern Homeland: The Report of the Mackenzie Valley Pipeline Inquiry*. Vol. 1. Ottawa: Department of Supply and Services, 1977.

Berton, Pierre. *Klondike: The Last Great Gold Rush*. Toronto: McClelland and Stewart, 1972.

———. *The Arctic Grail: The Quest for the Northwest Passage and the North Pole, 1818–1909*. Toronto: McClelland and Stewart, 1988.

Black, Martha. *My Ninety Years*. Anchorage: Alaska Northwest Publishing, 1976.

Blondin, George, ed. *When the World Was New: Stories of the Sahtu Dene*. Yellowknife: Outcrop, 1990.

Bockstoce, J.R. *Steam Whaling in the Western Arctic*. New Bedford: Old Dartmouth Historical Society, 1977.

Bone, Robert. *The Geography of the Canadian North: Issues and Challenges*. Toronto: Oxford University Press, 1992.

Bray, E.F. *A Frenchman in Search of Franklin*. Toronto: University of Toronto Press, 1992.

Breynat, Msgr G. *Cinquante Ans au Pays des Neiges*. 3 vols. Montreal: Fides, 1945–48.

Brody, Hugh, *Maps and Dreams*. Vancouver: Douglas and McIntyre, 1981.

———. *The Living Arctic*. Vancouver: Douglas and McIntyre, 1987.

Camsell, C. *Son of the North*. Toronto: Ryerson, 1954.

Coates, K.S. *Best Left as Indians: Native–White Relations in the Yukon Territory, 1840–1973*. Montreal: McGill-Queen's University Press, 1991.

Coates, K.S., and W.R. Morrison. *Land of the Midnight Sun: A History of the Yukon*. Edmonton: Hurtig, 1988.

———. *The Sinking of the Princess Sophia: Taking the North Down With Her*. Toronto: Oxford University Press, 1990; Fairbanks: University of Alaska Press, 1991.

———. *The Alaska Highway in World War II: The American Army of Occupation in Canada's Northwest*. Norman: University of Oklahoma Press; Toronto: University of Toronto Press, 1992.

———. *The Forgotten North*. Toronto: James Lorimer, 1992.

Coates, K.S., and W.R. Morrison, eds. *For Purposes of Dominion: Essays in Honour of Morris Zaslow*. Toronto: Captus University Press, 1989.

———. *Interpreting Canada's North: Selected Readings*. Toronto: Copp Clark, 1989.

Cody, H.A. *An Apostle of the North: Memoirs of the Right Reverend William Carpenter Bompas, DD*. Toronto: Musson, 1908.

Cooke, Alan, and C. Holland. *The Exploration of Northern Canada*. Toronto: Arctic History Press, 1978.

Crnkovich, Mary, ed. *Gossip: A Spoken History of*

Women in the North. Ottawa: Canadian Arctic Resources Committee (CARC), 1990.

Cruikshank, Julie. *Life Lived Like a Story: Life Stories of Three Yukon Native Elders.* Vancouver: University of British Columbia Press, 1990.

Dacks, Gurston. *A Choice of Futures.* Toronto: Methuen, 1981.

Daniels, Roy. *Alexander Mackenzie and the North West.* London: Faber and Faber, 1969.

Dawson, G.M. *Report on an Exploration in the Yukon District, N.W.T. and Adjacent Northern Portion of British Columbia, 1887.* Ottawa: King's Printer, 1888.

Dickason, Olive P. *Canada's First Nations: A History of Founding Peoples from Earliest Times.* 2nd edn. Toronto: Oxford University Press, 1997.

Diubaldo, R.J. *Stefansson and the Canadian Arctic.* Montreal: McGill-Queen's University Press, 1978.

Fagan, Brian M. *The Great Journey: The Peopling of North America.* New York: Thames and Hudson, 1987.

Fairley, T.C. *Sverdrup's Arctic Adventures.* London: Longmans, 1959.

Finnie, O.S. *Canada Moves North.* Toronto: Macmillan, 1942.

Francis, Daniel. *Discovery of the North: The Exploration of Canada.* Edmonton: Hurtig, 1986.

Freuchen, Peter. *Book of the Eskimos.* Greenwich, CT: Fawcett Crest, 1961.

Fumoleau, René. *As Long as this Land Shall Last: A History of Treaties 8 and 11.* Toronto: McClelland and Stewart, 1973.

Geiger, John, and Owen Beattie. *Frozen in Time: Unlocking the Secrets of the Franklin Expedition.* Saskatoon: Western Producer, 1988.

——. *Dead Silence: The Greatest Mystery in Arctic Discovery.* Toronto: Viking, 1993.

Grant, John W. *Moon of Wintertime: Missionaries and Indians of Canada in Encounter Since 1534.* Toronto: University of Toronto Press, 1984.

Grant, Shelagh. *Sovereignty or Security?: Government Policy in the Canadian North, 1936–1950.* Vancouver: University of British Columbia Press, 1988.

Green, Lewis. *The Gold Hustlers.* Vancouver: J.J. Douglas, 1972.

Hamelin, L.-E. *Canadian Nordicity: It's Your North Too.* Trans. W. Barr. Montreal: Harvest House, 1978.

Hearne, Samuel. *A Journey From Prince of Wales's Fort in Hudson's Bay to the Northern Ocean.* Richard Glover, ed. Toronto: Macmillan, 1958.

Helm, June, ed. *Handbook of North American Indians.* Vol. 6. *Subarctic Indians.* Washington: Smithsonian Institution, 1981.

Holmes, Douglas. *Northerners: Profiles of People in the Northwest Territories.* Toronto: James Lorimer, 1989.

Ives, John W. *A Theory of Northern Athapaskan Prehistory.* Calgary: University of Calgary Press, 1990.

Jenness, Diamond. *Eskimo Administration II: Canada.* Montreal: Arctic Institute of North America, 1964.

Jenness, Stuart, ed. *Arctic Odyssey: The Diary of Diamond Jenness.* Ottawa: Canadian Museum of Civilization, 1991.

Karamanski, Theodore. *Fur Trade and Exploration: Opening the Far Northwest, 1821–1852.* Vancouver: University of British Columbia Press, 1978.

King, Richard. *The Franklin Expedition from First to Last.* London: Churchill, 1855.

Lamb, W. Kaye, ed. *The Journals and Letters of Sir Alexander Mackenzie.* Cambridge: Cambridge University Press, 1970.

Larsen, Henry. *The Big Ship.* Toronto: McClelland and Stewart, 1967.

Lee, H.P. *Policing the Top of the World.* London: John Lane, 1928.

Lopez, Barry. *Arctic Dreams: Imagination and Desire in a Northern Landscape.* New York: Charles Scribner's Sons, 1986.

Lotz, Jim. *Northern Realities: The Future of Northern Development in Canada.* Toronto: New Press, 1972.

Lysyk, K., et al. *Alaska Highway Pipeline Inquiry.* Ottawa: Supply and Services Canada, 1977.

McClellan, Catharine, et al. *Part of the Land, Part of the Water: A History of the Yukon Indians.* Vancouver: Douglas and McIntyre, 1987.

McCullum, Hugh. *This Land is Not for Sale.* Toronto: Anglican Book Centre, 1975.

Mackenzie, Sir Alexander. *Voyages . . . to the Frozen and Pacific Oceans . . . .* London: Cadell and Davies, 1801.

Maclaren, I.S. 'The Aesthetic Map of the North'. In Coates and Morrison, eds, *Interpreting Canada's North: Selected Readings.*

McMahon, K. *Arctic Twilight: Reflections on the Destiny of Canada's Northern Land and People.* Toronto: Lorimer, 1988.

Metayer, Maurice, trans. *I, Nuligak.* New York: Pocket Books, 1971.

Morison, S.E. *The European Discovery of America: The Northern Voyages A.D. 500–1600.* New York: Oxford University Press, 1971.

Morrison, W.R. *Showing the Flag: The Mounted Police and Canadian Sovereignty in the North, 1894–1925.* Vancouver: University of British Columbia Press, 1985.

Morrison, W.R., and K.S. Coates. *Working the North: Labor and the Northwest Defense Projects, 1942–1945.* Fairbanks: University of Alaska Press, 1994.

Moss, John. *Enduring Dreams: An Exploration of Arctic Landscape.* Don Mills, ON: Anansi, 1994.

Mowat, Farley. *People of the Deer.* Boston: Little, Brown, 1952.

——. *The Desperate People.* Boston: Little, Brown, 1959.

Moyles, R.G. *British Law and Arctic Men.* Saskatoon: Western Producer Prairie Books, 1979.

Neatby, Leslie. *The Search for Franklin.* Edmonton: Hurtig, 1970.

North, Dick. *The Lost Patrol.* Anchorage, Alaska: Northwest Publishing, 1978.

North, Dick. *The Mad Trapper of Rat River.* Toronto: Macmillan, 1972.

Ogilvie, William. *Early Days on the Yukon & the Story of its Gold Finds.* Ottawa: Thorburn and Abbott, 1913.

Page, Robert. *Northern Development: The Canadian Dilemma.* Toronto: McClelland and Stewart, 1986.

Peake, F.A. *The Bishop Who Ate His Boots: A Biography of Isaac O. Stringer.* Don Mills, ON: Anglican Church of Canada, 1966.

Petrone, Penny. *Northern Voices: Inuit Writing in English.* Toronto: University of Toronto Press, 1988.

Phillips, R.A.J. *Canada's North.* Toronto: Macmillan, 1967.

Pitseolak, Peter, and Dorothy Eber. *People From Our Side.* Montreal: McGill-Queen's University Press, 1993.

Rea, K.J. *The Political Economy of the Canadian North.* Toronto: University of Toronto Press, 1968.

Rich, E.E. *The History of the Hudson's Bay Company, 1670–1870.* London: Hudson's Bay Record Society, 1958-59.

Robertson, Gordon. *Northern Provinces: A Mistaken Goal?* Ottawa: Institute of Public Policy Research, 1986.

Ross, W.G., ed. *An Arctic Whaling Diary: The Journal of Captain George Comer in Hudson Bay, 1903–1905.* Toronto: University of Toronto Press, 1984.

Sahlins, M. *Stone Age Economics.* New York: Aldine de Gruyter, 1972.

Steele, S.B. *Forty Years in Canada.* London: Jenkins, 1915.

Stefansson, V. *My Life with the Eskimo.* New York: Macmillan, 1913.

——. *Discovery.* New York: McGraw-Hill, 1964.

——. *The Friendly Arctic.* New York: Macmillan, 1921.

Sverdrup, O. *New Land: Four Years in the Arctic Regions.* 2 vols. London: Longmans Green, 1904.

Tester, Frank J., and Peter Kulchyski. *Tammarniit (Mistakes): Inuit Relocation in the Eastern Arctic, 1939–63.* Vancouver: University of British Columbia Press, 1994.

VanStone, James. *Athapaskan Adaptations: Hunters and Fishermen of the Subarctic Forests.* Chicago: Aldine, 1975.

Webb, Melody. *The Last Frontier: A History of the Yukon Basin of Canada and Alaska.* Albuquerque: University of New Mexico Press, 1985.

Woodman, David. *Unravelling the Franklin Mystery: Inuit Testimony.* Montreal: McGill-Queen's University Press, 1991.

Wright, A.A. *Prelude to Bonanza: The Discovery and Exploration of the Yukon*. Whitehorse: Arctic Star Printing, 1980.

Young, Steven B. *To The Arctic: An Introduction to the Far Northern World*. New York: John Wiley, 1989.

Yukon Native Brotherhood. *Together Today for our Children Tomorrow*. Whitehorse: Yukon Native Brotherhood, 1973.

Zaslow, Morris. *The Opening of the Canadian North, 1870–1914*. Toronto: McClelland and Stewart, 1971.

——. *The Northward Expansion of Canada, 1914–1967*. Toronto: McCelland and Stewart, 1988.

——, ed. *A Century of Canada's Arctic Islands 1880–1890*. Ottawa: Royal Society of Canada, 1981.

INDEX

PLEASE NOTE: Page numbers in italic type refer to illustration captions.

Abel, Kerry, 58

Aklavik, NWT, 10, 60, 117

Alaska, 46, 50

Alaska Commercial Company, 50, 79, 89

Alaska Highway, 5, 126, 134, 148, 150–1, 172; cost, 137; environmental effects, 137–8; purpose, 132

Alert, NWT, 164

Alikomiak, 122

Alyeska pipeline, 168–9

Amund Ringnes Island, 74

Amundsen, Roald, 72, 73–4

Anglican missionaries: attitudes towards Native people, 56; and class, 57; and Roman Catholic missionaries, 56

Annegolok, Paulette, *51*

Athabaska River, 45; Lake, 45, 67

Athapaskan peoples, 21–2, 25–6; pre-contact life, 26–9

Aviation, 125–6, 148, 165; Northwest Staging Route, 130–1, 133

Axel Heiberg Island, 3–4, 31, 74

'Baby bonus'. *See* Mothers' Allowance

Bache Peninsula, NWT, 118

Baffin Island, 38, 40

Baffin, Thomas, 42

Barrenlands, 15, 157

Basques, 38

Bastedo, Jamie, 15–16

Bell, John, 47

Bella Coola River, 68

Bennett Lake, 96, *157*

Berger, Carl, 2, 8

Berger, Thomas, 171, *178* ; *see also* Mackenzie Valley pipeline inquiry

Bering Strait 'land bridge' theory, 18, 19, 29

Bernier, J.E., 118

Berrigan, Martin, 145

Berry, Clarence, 7

Berton, Pierre, 79, 167

Black, George, 95, 185, 186

Black, Martha, 94–5, *184*, 185

Blackwater Group, 186

Blair, Bob, 174

Blondin-Andrew, Ethel, 184

Bloody Falls, 65, *66*

Bompas, Bishop W.C., *54*, 56, 57, 59

Bonanza Creek, 87, 88, 89, *91, 93,* 106; *see also* Klondike

Borden Island, 75, 105

Boyle, 'Klondike Joe', 107, 108

Brintnell, Leigh, 126

Broken Hill Properties, 186

Buchanan, Judd, 182

Cabot, John, 38

Caesar, Louis, 173

Cambridge Bay, NWT, 165

Campbell, Robert, 47–8

Camsell, Charles, 8

'Canada First' movement, 8

Canadian Arctic Expedition (1913–18), 62, 75–6, 105

Canadian Arctic Gas Pipeline Ltd, 170–1

Canadian Encyclopedia, 171

Canadian Pacific Airlines, 126

Canadian Pacific Railway, 13

Canadian Shield, 13–16

Canham, T.H., *53*

Canol project, 126, 133, 134–7, 140, 148–9, 151

Cape Dorset, NWT, *4, 7,* 31

Cape Dyer, NWT, 165

Cape Fullerton, NWT, 117

Cape Perry, NWT, 165

Cape Wolstenholme, NWT, *60*

Carcross, YT, *103,* 156; residential school, *59,* 60, 61

Carmack, George, 86–8

Cartier, Jacques, 41, 186

Catton, W.E., 126

Charlie, Johnny, *180*

Charles, HRH Prince, *180*

Charman, Frank, *85*

Chesterfield Inlet, NWT, 51

Chilkoot Pass, *81–5,* 91, 92, 93–4, 96; 'the Scales', 94; Sheep Camp, 94

Chipewyan, 28–9, 64, 67

Chrétien, Jean, *169*

Churchill, Man., 10, 12, 44

Coates, Ken, ix, 26–7

Cold War, 164

Columbus, Christopher, 36, 38

Cominco Ltd, *108,* 162

Committee for Original People's Entitlement (COPE), 182

Conservation, 141

Consolidated Gold Mine, 126

Constantine, Charles, *80,* 115, 116

Coppermine, NWT, 51

Coppermine River, 64

Council for Yukon Indians, 178

Craig Harbour, NWT, 118, 159–60

Cree, 64

Crozier, Captain Francis, 71–2

Cumberland House, 66

Davis, John, 42

Dawson Charlie (Tagish Charlie), 86, 87

Dawson, George M., 88

Dawson City, YT, *90–7,* 78, 88, 90, *92, 96–7,* 147–8, *156, 166–7, 171;* gold rush era, 98–9, 101; Guggieville, 83; routes to, 90–7 (*see also* Chilkoot; White Pass)

Dawson Creek, BC, 143

Defence projects, wartime, 130–51; and Canadian sovereignty, 142–4; Cold War period, 164–6; effects on Native people, 137–42; effects on northern communities, 144–8; environmental effects, 139–41; policing, 143–4; surplus goods and equipment, 149–50; *see also* Alaska Highway; Canol

Dempster Highway, 161

Dempster patrol, *120*

Dene, 7, 56, 58–9, 61, 122, 183; 'Dene Declaration' (1975), 181–2; language, 21–2; and Mackenzie Valley pipeline inquiry, 173; treaties, 111–12, 152

Denendeh, 188

Dictionary of Canadian Biography, 72

Diefenbaker, John, 11, 160–2, 165

Distant Early Warning (DEW) line, 164, 165, 166

Doak, W.A., 122

Dorset culture, 31–3

Dyea, Alaska, 92, 94

Edmonton, Alta, 91, 144, 148, 175–6, 187–8; 'Klondike Days', 91

Eldorado Creek, 88, 89

Ellef Ringnes Island, 3–4, 74

Ellesmere Island, 29, 31, 159, 160

Ennadai Lake, 51, 54

Eric the Red, 37

Ericsson, Leif, 37–8

Eureka, NWT, 164

'Exercise Musk-Ox', 164

Exploration, 2, 4, 37–43, 62–77; motives for, 62; Norse, 37–8; pre-Columbian, 37; *see also* Fur trade

Faro, YT, 162, 188

Fitzgerald, F.J., 116, *117,* 119–20

Fitzgerald, Alta, 148

Foothills Pipe Lines project, 174–5

Fort Albany, Ont., 44

Fort Chipewyan, Alta, 67

Fort Good Hope, NWT, 45
Fort Liard, NWT, 154
Fort McPherson, NWT, 45, 68, 116, 154
Fort Nelson, BC, 92, 148
Fort Norman, NWT, 68, 148
Fort Prince of Wales, 44, 64
Fort Providence, NWT, 148
Fort Reliance, 79
Fort Selkirk, 48
Fort Simpson, NWT, 45, 68, 148, 154
Fort Smith, NWT, *110,* 148, 154, 177
Fort Youcon (Yukon), *46, 47,* 48, 49
Fortymile, YT, 79–80, 87–8
Foster, W.W., 143
Franklin, Sir John, 68–72; last expedition, 70–2, 73
Fraser River, 68
French, Alice (Masak), 61
Frobisher, Martin, 2, *37,* 39–42
Frobisher Bay (Iqaluit), *15,* 148, 154, 165, 184
Fumoleau, Father René, 61, 173
Fur trade, 13–14, 44–54; inter-war period, 124; and Inuit, 51–4; Montreal traders, 44–5, 64, 67; Native middlemen, 46–7, 48, 52; trade goods, 45, 49, 50; *see also* Hudson's Bay Company; North West Company

Gander, Nfld, 148
Geological Survey of Canada, 88
Glaciers, 18–19
Gold: placer (alluvial), 83; value of, 88, 89, 108, 125
Gold mining, 162, 186; financing, 107; mining techniques, 79, 82–6, 106–8, 109; Yellowknife area, 82, 125; *see also* Klondike
Gold rushes, 78; *see also* Klondike
Goose Bay, Nfld, 148
Grant, John Webster, 58
Great Bear Lake, 124, 126
Great Slave Lake, 67, 126
Green, Peter, *174*
Greenland, 30–1, 33
Grinnell, Henry, 72
Guggenheim family, 107
Gwitch'in, 26, 28, 56; *see also* Athapaskan peoples

Hall Beach, NWT, 165

Hall, Charles Francis, 41
Hamelin, L.-E., 11
Hamilton, Alvin, 161
Han, 26
Hanbury River, NWT, *12*
Hardy, Louise, 186
Harper, Arthur, 78–9
Hay River, NWT, *57, 60,* 120
Hearne, Samuel, 62, 63–6
Herschel Island, *5,* 112, 113–14, 116, 117
Holland, Clive, 72
Hudson, Henry, 43
Hudson Strait, 42
Hudson's Bay Company, 109, 124; charter, 44; competitors, 44–5, 51; and Samuel Hearne, 64; on Herschel Island, 117; merger with North West Company, 45, 68; and missionaries, 55–6; *see also* Fur trade
Humboldt, Alexander von, 36–7
Hunker Creek, YT, *89*

Igloolik Education Society, 187
Imperial Oil Company, 126
Ingstad, Helge, 38
Inside Passage, 123
Inuit, 130; art, 7; 'blond Eskimos', 75; and Canadian law, 121, 122; culture, 34–5; and early explorers, 41; employment, 165; in fur trade, 51–4, 124; Inuvialuit, 182 (*see also* Nunavut); language, 22; and Norse, 38; oral history, 32; origins, 20, 29, 30–4; relocation program, 159–60; and whalers, 114–15; urbanization, 164; *see also* Dorset culture; Palaeo-Eskimos; Thule culture
Inuit Cultural Institute, 187
Inuit Tapirisat, 182, 187
Inukshuit, 1, *35*
Inuvik, 154
Iqaluit, 148, 154, 165, *170,* 184
Isachsen, NWT, 164
Isotherms, 10
Ives, J.W., 22

Jarvis, Inspector A.M., 52–3
Jeckell, George, 129
Johns, Johnny, 61

Johnson, Albert, 122, 126

Kalluak, Mark, *165*
Kaningoak, Peter, *30*
Karetak-Lindell, Nancy, 185
Karluk expedition, 76
Kaska, 26
Kaskawulsh Glacier, *11*
Keenleyside, Hugh, 8–9
Keewatin, 6, 12, 15
King, W.L. Mackenzie, 152
King William Island, 71
Kirkland Lake, Ont., 14
Klondike gold rush, 5, 7, 78–103; end of, 102; gold
   production, 102–3, 108; timing of, 82; *see also*
   Gold; Gold mining
Klondike Mines Railway, 102
Kluane National Park, 2, 11, 141–2
Knuth, Eigil, 29
Koaha, Suzie, *179*
Kunuk, Methuselah, *158*
Kutchin. *See* Gwitch'in

Laberge, Lake, *87*
Labine, Gilbert, 124–5, 126
Lac de Gras, YT, 186
Ladue, Joe, 88
Lake Harbour, NWT, *10,* 51, 118, *162*
Lamson and Hubbard, 124
Lapierre's House, 47
Larsen, Henry, *74*
La Vérendrye, Pierre Gaultier de Varennes et de, 44
Le Roux, Father, 121
Leslie, Frank, 80–2
Lindbergh, Charles and Anne, *127*
Lindeman, Lake, *86,* 93–4, 96
Lindner, Sonny, *175*
Locke, Leonard, 123
Lok, Michael, 41
London, Jack, 95–6
Lopez, Barry, 12
Loucheux, 56
Lovett Gulch, YT, *106*
Lynn Canal, 92, 124
Lysyk, Kenneth, 174

L'Anse aux Meadows, Nfld, 38

McClellan, Catharine, 22–5
McConachie, Grant, 126
Macdonald, John A., 160–1, 162
Macdonald, Malcolm, 142
McGhee, Robert, 29–30
Mackenzie, Sir Alexander, 45, 66–8, *67*
Mackenzie Highway, 161–2
Mackenzie King Island, 75
Mackenzie River, 45, 67–8, 126
Mackenzie Valley pipeline, 61, 170–1; inquiry,
   171–3, 181
Maclaren, I.S., 1
McLaughlin, Audrey, 186
McQuesten, Leroy Napoleon 'Jack', 78
'Mad trapper' of Rat River, 122, 126
Malaspina Glacier, 91
Manhattan incident, 7
Masak (Alice French), 61
Matonabbee, 64–5, 66
May, W.R. 'Wop', 126
Mayo, Arthur, 79
Mayo, YT, *99,* 109
Meighen Island, 3–4, 75, 105
Melville Island, 118
Methye Portage, 45, 67
Métis, 173, 182, 183
'Mid-Canada' concept, 11
'Mid-Canada line', 165
Miles Canyon, *13,* 94, 97
Miners' meeting, 80–2, 87
Mining, 188; asbestos, 163; copper, 108–9, 163;
   diamond, 186; effects on NWT, 126–7; lead-zinc,
   109, 162; radium, 124–5; silver, 109; *see also* Gold
   mining
Missionaries, 4, 54–61, 115–16, 121; and HBC,
   55–6; *see also* Anglican missionaries; Roman
   Catholic missionaries; Schools, mission
Moosenose, Marie, 173
Morison, Samuel Eliot, 36, 38
Mothers' Allowance, 153
Mould Bay, NWT, 164
Mounted Police, 112; in Arctic, 116–17, 118, 119;
   'Lost Patrol', 119–20; opinions of Native peoples,

52; in Yukon, 91–2, 94, 98–9; *see also* Royal
    Canadian Mounted Police
Mount Logan, 2
Mowat, Farley, 6, 157–8, 160
Munro, John, *174*
Murray, Alexander Hunter, 47

Nansen, Fridtjof, 72, 73, 74
National Film Board, 7, 164
Native people: education, 152, 153–6 (*see also* Schools,
    mission); and fur trade, 46–7, 48–50, 52, 53–4, 104;
    health care, 152, 158; and Klondike gold rush,
    103–4, 109; land claims, 173, 178–84; languages,
    18, 19, 21–2, 187–8; and Mackenzie Valley pipeline
    inquiry, 172–3; and missionaries, 54–61; and
    Mothers' Allowance, 3; oral history, 24; origins,
    17–20; political empowerment, 175–6, 177–8, 187;
    and popular images of North, 7; population, 20–1,
    109, 127; spirituality, 27, 31–2, 57–9; treaties,
    111–12, 152, 179, 181; urbanization, 164; and
    wartime defence projects, 137–40; and White Paper
    on Indian Policy, 157, 177–8; *see also* Athapaskan
    peoples; Dene; Inuit; Métis
New Democratic Party, 177
Nielsen, Erik, 185–6
Njootli, Amos, *53*
Nome, Alaska, 102
Nordicity, 11–12
Norman Wells, NWT, 111, 126, 133, 148
Norse, 37–8
North: and British imperialism, 8; and Canadian
    nationalism, 8–9; climate, 10–12, 15; as frontier,
    2–3, 7, 9, 61, 78, 122; as homeland, 2, 3, 7, 61,
    187, 188; 'northernness', 9–12; popular images of,
    1–2, 4–7; size, 3, 12; tourism, 166–7; *see also*
    Northwest Territories; Yukon
Northern Trading Company, 124
North Pole, 62
North West Company, 44–5, 68
Northwest Passage, 7, 39, 42, 62, 64, 67, 69, 70, 73
Northwest Territories, 9, 106; boundaries, 105;
    communications, 148, 151; government, 127–8,
    176–7; partition of, *see* Nunavut; population, 12,
    127, 130, 154, 163; representation in Parliament,
    184–5; urbanization, 164

Norton, Moses, 64
Nuligak, 115
Nunavut, 148, 182–4

'O Canada', 8
Oil and gas industry, 163, 168–71; exploration,
    169–70; *see also* Mackenzie Valley pipeline
Oil spills, 169
Old Age Pension, 157
Old Crow, YT, 50, 178
Oliver, Frank, 60, 61, 111
Oomak, Thomas, *52*
Organization of Petroleum Exporting Countries
    (OPEC), 168

Padloping Island, 154
Palaeo-Eskimos, 29–30
Pangnirtung, NWT, 51, *116*, 118, *119*
Parkin, George, 8
Peace River, 68
Peary, Robert, 5, 7, 72
Peel's River Post (Fort McPherson), 45, 47
Penikett, Tony, *177*, 181
Permafrost, 84–5, 140, 171–2
Pine Point, NWT, 161, 162, 188
'Pinetree line', 165
Pitseolak, Peter, 32–4
'Polar values' index (VAPO), 11–12
Pond, Peter, 67
Pond Inlet, NWT, *6, 58*, 118, 159
Port Radium, NWT, 125, 126
Povungnituk, Que., 7
Prince Charles Island, 105–6
Prince Rupert, BC, 148
Princess Sophia, 122–4, *125*

Quaker Oats Company, 166–7
Quebec, British conquest of, 44

Radford, H.V., 120–1
Rampart House, 50
Raymond, Charles, 50
Resolute, NWT, 159, 164
Revillon Frères, 51, 109, 124
Rich, E.E., 67

Richardson Mountains, 136

Roads to Resources program, 161

Rocky Mountains, 14

Rogers, Stan, 72

Rohmer, Richard, 11

Roman Catholic missionaries, 55; attitudes towards Native people, 56; *see also* Schools, mission

Rouvière, Father, 121

Royal Canadian Mounted Police (RCMP), 120, 160; and 'mad trapper', 122; in Yukon, 143–4

Rupert's Land, 110

Sadlermuit, 33

Sahlins, Marshall, 26

Schefferville, Que., 14

Schools, mission: day/seasonal, 60–1; government support for, 59; residential, 59–60, 155–6, 173; 'mission school syndrome', 156

Scott, Sir Robert, 69, 71, 74

Service, Robert, 100–2

Shamee, Lillian, *181*

Shea, Dolphus, 173

Sidney, Angela, 17, 187

Sinnisiak, 121

Skagway, Alaska, 92–3, 94, 96, 102

Skookum Jim, 86, 87

Smith, Soapy, 92, 93

Snowshoe, John, *163*

Social welfare, 152–60

Southampton Island, 33

Sovereignty, Canadian, 98, 110–11, 112, 114, 117, 118, 142–4

St Laurent, Louis, 152

Steele, Samuel B., 69, *88*, 92–3, 98

Stefansson, Vilhjalmur, 62, 73, 74–7, 105, 130, 131

Stewart River, 80

Strategic Air Command, 165

Street, George, 120–1

Stringer, Isaac O., 115–16

Sudbury, Ont., 14

Sutherland, F.D., 116

Sverdrup, Otto, 72, 73, 74, 105

Swinton, George, 32

Tabac, Georgina, 173

Tagish, 26

Tagish Charlie (Dawson Charlie), 86, 87

Tammarniit ('Mistakes'), 160

Teslin, YT, 60, 138

Teslin Lake, 92

Thule culture, 31, 33–4

Tlingit, 26, 48

Treadgold, A.N.C, 107

Tree line, 10

Tuktoyaktuk, NWT, 163

Tutcho, Susie, 173

Tutchone, 26

Uluksuk, 121

US Army Corps of Engineers, 134

US Public Roads Administration, 134

VanStone, James, 26

VAPO ('polar values' index), 11–12

Victoria Island, 75

Vittrekwa, Peter, *163*

Waterways, Alta, 148

Watkins, Mel, 173

Watson Lake, NWT, 148

Weather stations, 164

Webster, Anne, *51*

Weir, Robert Stanley, 8

Western Canadian Airways, 126

Whale Island, 67

Whaling, 112–13, 117

White Paper on Indian Policy (1969), 157, 177–8

White Pass, 91, 92, 95–6; Dead Horse Gulch, 95–6

White Pass and Yukon Railway (WP&YR), 93, 102, 103, 146

White River ash fall, 25

Whitehorse, YT, 10, 93, *100*, 102, 133, *139*, 143, 145, 146–8, 151, *161*

Whittaker, C.E., 116

Wood, Frederick, 128

Woodman, Dave, 72

Wrangel Island, 75

Yakutat Bay, 91

Yellowknife, NWT, 14, 82, *111*, 125, 126–7, *154*;

Corrections Institute, *176;* Prince of Wales Northern Heritage Centre, *180;* territorial capital, 176

York Factory, 44

Yukon, 9, 15, 106; capital, 148, 176; communications, 102, 105, 133, 148, 151; government, 98, 128–9, 177, 180–1; mining, 162–3; policing, 98–9, 102; population, 12, 98, 102, 103, 105, 106, 109, 122, 124, 130; representation in Parliament, 184–6; Territorial Council, 98, 128; territorial status, 98; western boundary treaty, 46

Yukon Consolidated Gold Co., 108, 162

Yukon Field Force, 98

Yukon Native Brotherhood, 178

Yukon River, 91, 92, 93, 102

Zaslow, Morris, ix